GROUSE
and Lesser Gods

GROUSE
and Lesser Gods

Ted Nelson Lundrigan

Illustrations by Bob White

THE DERRYDALE PRESS
Lanham • Boulder • New York • London

THE DERRYDALE PRESS

Published by The Derrydale Press
An imprint of The Rowman & Littlefield Publishing Group, Inc.
4501 Forbes Boulevard, Suite 200, Lanham, Maryland 20706
www.rowman.com

Unit A, Whitacre Mews, 26–34 Stannary Street, London SE11 4AB

Distributed by NATIONAL BOOK NETWORK

Text Copyright © 2002, 2015 by Ted Nelson Lundrigan
Illustrations Copyright © 2002, 2015 by Ted Nelson Lundrigan
First Derrydale Printing 2015

Dust jacket and interior design by Lynda H. Mills

ISBN 978-0-89272-588-5 (cloth : alk. paper)—ISBN 978-1-58667-140-2
(pbk.: alk. paper)—ISBN 978-1-60893-079-1 (electronic)

Library of Congress Control Number: 2002114280

∞™ The paper used in this publication meets the minimum requirements of
American National Standard for Information Sciences—Permanence of Paper
for Printed Library Materials, ANSI/NISO Z39.48-1992.

Printed in the United States of America

— *Dedication* —

To my English setter Salty
and to my Labrador retriever Dixie,
who together taught me everything
I know about bird hunting

— *Table of Contents* —

Preface

I have never met Ted Nelson Lundrigan. Nor have I set foot in north-central Minnesota, where he lives.

But I have hunted with him there many times. I have admired the bird work of his big, lean German shorthair, Beans. I have sunk to my knees in a black-mud hole that lay unseen in an alder thicket, emerging to peals of laughter from Ted. I have sat silently with him in a small church graveyard, trying to understand why a beautiful baby girl left this world before she had a chance to savor its wonders. And I have watched Ted's intensity build in a productive grouse covert until his every movement was a marvel of precision.

All this—and much more—was possible because I read Ted's excellent first book, *Hunting the Sun,* and because he graciously let me work on this equally special second volume, *Grouse and Lesser Gods.*

Even without meeting him, I know that Ted is a generous person. Otherwise, he would have kept most of the thoughts, experiences, places, and people in these books to himself. Instead, he has shared them with us—openly, frankly, and with a style and grace that set him apart as a writer of bird-hunting tales. I, along with literally thousands of other readers, are much the better for his generosity.

Like most grouse hunters, I have never experienced a forty-flush day, the kind of day where birds are exploding so often that your heart starts beating irregularly and your arm begins to hurt like hell because you keep failing to get the butt of the gun tucked into your shoulder where it belongs. The kind of day when your setter or pointer is confronted with so much scent that he doesn't know which way to turn first.

I can't say that this never happens in Maine, where I live and hunt birds, but it certainly hasn't ever happened to me. Ted Lundrigan, however, knows about forty-flush days, because he has experienced them. Many times. Part of that is because he lives in (and even owns) some of the nation's most productive ruffed grouse country. But in my opinion, the reason Ted sees so many grouse is because these wild, thundering birds are absolutely, positively his life's passion. As a result, he has become very, very good at hunting them.

But if you have read *Hunting the Sun,* you already know that. What you don't know is the story behind this second book, the one you're now holding in your hands. As Ted's editor, I need to tell it.

He created the initial draft of this manuscript three years ago. Because book publishers come, languish, and go, it never saw the light of day. After the company I work for bought Countrysport Press, *Grouse and Lesser Gods* eventually found its way to my desk. By that time, readers were clamoring for "Ted's new book," and he was understandably impatient to see it in print.

So I read it. Twice. There were some wonderful chapters and some not-so-wonderful chapters. In my opinion, the whole thing didn't "hang together." So I wrote Ted a long, carefully worded letter explaining what I thought were the problems that needed additional attention. Needless to say, he was disappointed and, frankly, pissed off, which I suspect is one of the character traits that make him a good attorney. He said he'd think about it.

About six months later, he sent me a letter in which he revealed that he was finally able to revisit the manuscript and that it pained him greatly to admit that I had been essentially correct in my analysis of its flaws. He said, "I'm going to start over. I'm going to make it right." That took a lot of guts. He could have said, "Screw you; I'm going to another publisher." But he didn't, and you're about to find out just how good Ted Lundrigan's writing can be. That he allowed me to be part of this process is something for which I am very grateful.

But, as my older daughter, Anne, would say, "Okay, I get the point! Enough is enough!"

It's time for you to go hunting with Ted in his beloved Promised Land and its environs. This is a magical place of rivers, of water. Of gun dogs and shotguns and ruffed grouse and bird dogs. Of dogwoods and birches and ferns and alders. Of Scandinavian farmers and aggressive cattle. Even of bears and wolves. Most important, it is a place of gods, both lesser and greater.

I have just two pieces of advice: First, watch where you step. Second, shoot fast. If you don't, Ted—generous though he is— will "wipe your eye" in a heartbeat.

Chris Cornell, Editor
Countrysport Press

THE
MISED
AND

BBY'S

MAYO

R

R

CREEK

North

CHAPTER ONE
The Reach of Rivers

Water reaches everywhere. It touches the past. It prepares the future. It moves under the ground and is drawn up through the roots, where it wanders—in the words of Loren Eiseley—thinly, in the heights of trees. It pulses in blood, part salt, part sun and time, sustaining life in the form of men, grouse, and green leaves.

It is absorbed by the nucleus of every cell, extending its shape by osmosis. It is at the heart of every appearance. The mother element, bringing into being nine-tenths of everything alive. Through its myriad puddles and streams, it creates a flying, bending, swishing projection of a water brotherhood in the leafy places where men and grouse wander. It is a way water has of going beyond the reach of its rivers.

The water I am moving along is a narrow, rocky tumble, haunted by years of memories, parts of myself that I have left here. It comes from the wrinkled frown of Maple Hill, formed to look down upon the neighboring fields when the last glacier pushed its load of earth and stone from Canada and trickled into Mayo Creek.

When that glacier dropped its old stones to form Maple Hill, it made a small continental divide. On the north side, Wood Row Creek, Goblin Creek, all the waters that nurture and create the bird covers of the Pedersen, the Creek Dogwoods, Uncle Willie's, and the Olson Brothers, flow northeast and east into the South Fork of the Pine River. From there, the water runs to Whitefish Lake and once again down the Pine into the Mississippi River. The Crow Wing River and the Mississippi meet just south of Brainerd, Minnesota, in what is now Crow Wing State Park.

A lot of history has been made at that junction, for it unites two trade routes, or so they told me when I was there. A battle was fought between the Dakota Sioux and the Ojibwa. Smoothbore trade muskets were fired from pits dug into the high banks. Every now and again a lead ball struck an enemy in a canoe or swimming about. The captive Indian women had turned over some of the canoes when the fireworks started. This event was not sufficiently explained, to my taste, but I was a Boy Scout when all this was revealed and therefore recall only the blood and thunder parts of the lecture. What I do remember quite clearly was the foreign look of the land there. It was oak trees in a ing brown dirt, and the water was broad and muddy. One or two of the more daring boys wanted to run at full speed off the bank, hoping to make it into the deep part of the river. I don't remember if it was good sense or the scoutmaster that prevailed, but the plan was abandoned in favor of just sitting and watching the river carve the border between the forest and the prairie.

That is what big rivers do best. They provide transportation. Like a metaphor for modern life, everything in them, or on them, is going somewhere. Each is a river of commerce, its freeways, turnpikes, and raceways moving to the sea as life passes by its window.

The really interesting water is only as wide as you can step across.

Walking along with me on this day is Tom Ferguson, a small, wiry man from Tennessee, made of the angles and bones that settled those mountains. We are hunting on flat land, as far as he is concerned, just a bit crowded by the brush and sticks. Our hunt has taken us along the edge of my little waterway, poking through the alder and golden swamp grass in the hope, vain up to this point, that a grouse would hide there. An obliging landowner has plowed a trail along his fence, ending in a pile of logs and dirt just short of the stream bank. It is a good place to rest and is of some historical significance, as I explain to him.

"This is Parker Buster Corner," I say, dusting the dirt off a barkless log.

He and I sit down.

"A few years ago my little setter dog, Salty, pointed a grouse right over there." I point to a clump of poplar sprouts.

"The first guy under the fence saw the point and walked over for the flush. I was just behind him but stayed on my side. The bird, a fine big red-tailed fellow, flushed up and straight away on the other side of the poplar. The shooter had a beautiful 16-gauge Parker side-by-side with a marbled, multicolored wooden stock."

"He missed and, at the same moment, bumped the gun against a nearby sapling. Then—and I swear to it, Tom, because I was there—he grabbed the barrels in one hand and the fore-end in the other, and swung the gun at the offending tree. He snapped the stock right off at the pistol grip."

"No!" Tom answers. "Git outta here!"

"God's truth," I say, raising my hand for an imaginary oath. "It swung there, back and forth, by the trigger tang."

"My Lord . . . what did he say?"

"He looked at it for a heartbeat or two and said, 'Ah broke mah gun.' He was also from the South, you know."

"That's it," Tom replies. "It's just a Yankee story."

"Nope," I answer, "it's the truth; my son was there and saw it, too. The guy put the gun under his arm, walked down this little hill behind us, and waded through that stream, called Mayo Creek. He went up to his knees, right through the middle of it."

"Why did he do that?" Tom asks, his eyes a little squinty in continuing disbelief.

"Don't know. Penance, I guess." Now inspired by waters, penance, baptism, and all, I pull on my revival minister's accent. "Like the good book says, through water ye shall be saved."

Tom leans forward, elbows on knees, and spits between his feet. "I'll go along with the gun, but y'all stretched that last part."

Then Tom reaches down and lifts a stone out of the dirt. It

is a little smaller than a cantaloupe, almost round and a deep green, like verdigris. He turns it over and over in his hands, cleaning the surface.

"Before I started my own company, I was a geologist," he states. "This is called serpentine, billions of years old, pushing to the surface only up on the Canadian shield. It was brought down by your last glacier. If I had my rock hammer, I'd break it open. Inside would be the prettiest green color you ever saw."

He passes it to me. It is heavy, way out of proportion to its size, and very close grained, almost smooth. I want to put it in my game bag to carry home. A rock that old ought not to be cast aside. But we have too far to walk, and, since I will come back and see it, from time to time, I leave it. It's in a good place, here on a log, next to Mayo Creek.

Like twin lines in God's palm, the Mayo has a companion, called North Mayo Creek, drawing its waters from another wrinkle in the brow of Maple Hill. It passes under the town road, only a culvert wide, less than half a mile from Tom's green rock. Brown stained by road dust and by ash and oak tannin, it is slowed a second time by the highway bridge. I can glance at it when I drive across. If the yellow grass shows its dark stain at the water mark, I will be able to ford the creek. If not, my hunt along those banks will be cut in half.

An errant drain of the glacier's ice cake took a trip south and created two lakes, then dried up. Water will find its way, and Stoney Brook broke out and redirected the errant flow to the southeast. For fifteen miles it seeps, tumbles, and flows, until it is finally able to slip around the back side of the high ground along the west shore of Upper Gull Lake, running into the same basin as the two Mayos. Stoney Brook is as far south as I care to go. It's not that there are no more good grouse covers south of Stoney, it's just that I can find everything I need between Stoney and the Mayos.

The little places are better, the places where the water slips over the stones with the sound of an astonished crowd. They have the feel of cold mornings and warm fires. When I push past the branches and look between the trees there are ghosts of men and women, the ghost dogs of friends. They are lined up waiting to see me, some in worn vests, some ahead, some waiting for me to pass by. On a rug in front of a brick fireplace a small white setter sleeps after its day in the fall sunlight. I see two little boys, my brother and I, jumping out of an old black '47 Chevrolet to run up the trail and see the bird our father swatted with a load of high-base No. 6 shot. Then we're running back to him, just as fast, to flee the grounded flutters of its last wingbeats.

I am a father now, myself, and, if I could, I would reach back and taste every element running through the rivers of that little boy I once was. First to sense what was in me before that bird beat its wings like a drum on the ground. Then, a heartbeat after those sounds flowed into my little boy soul, to find, with my tongue, the mineral, synapse, or neuron that became the passion of hunting. I would isolate it, refine it, and in a quiet moment, place its one shining drop on the tongue of each of my children, thereby ensuring I will remain forever with them in the shape of this memory.

I think of it, that one single grouse, its life having a predictable end devoid of old age. Like a flower rising from a bulb in the spring and dying with autumn's killing frost, the individual life over, but the garden continuing on. Populations are long lived, though most of the individuals will change from year to year. The birds will continue so long as the conditions where they live are suitable. A stream of water, wide enough to step across, is the guarantee.

I think of another river, a flow of time and experiences, the one I carry inside of me now and tend carefully. On a walk beside the Mayos and Stoney Brook, and within the other, that one inside me, I will visit the places I know and the places I knew. That walk will avoid the big rivers, covering only as much water as I can step across. The valleys of the Mayos and the Stoney are not trade routes. They have nothing to hinder the headlong flow of the world. Here the water has, indeed, become the green leafy branches, the grouse, and the men that hunt them. All things only, but a way that water has of going beyond the reach of rivers and between the trees.

CHAPTER TWO
The Source

There is a green hill of hard-oak ridges and poplar bottoms. It rises almost as high as Maple Hill. On one of its sides, the rush of Wood Row Creek has carved a valley between it and the Pedersen farm. The green hill is as stubborn as its taller companion. For eons the water has tried to cut its way through this hill into the source of Mayo Brook, and, for a like amount of time, the rocks and till have turned it aside. The Pedersens settled on their side of the green hill, and they, with their neighbors, built the First Norwegian Lutheran church on the Maple Hill side. Mayo Brook began to ooze its way south between the green hill and Maple Hill, keeping the ground too wet for trees.

A cartway was made. From the corner of the town road at the Pedersen farm it passed through a small field, now marked by the discarded hulk of a Minneapolis Moline tractor, and down through the watercourse of Wood Row Creek.

The two-rut trail crossed the creek, and for years the beavers tried to use the roadbed as a dam. It was a perfect choke point of trees and gravel. The Pedersens and the town road crew beat the beavers back. But nature is patient as well as persistent, and when the last of the Pedersens left the homestead, the stumpy hay meadow became a pond, and the roadbed was incorporated into a dam of sticks and mud.

It was a big drainage. The beavers had to work, and the extent of their labor reached high as well as long. When it was done, a large berm of wood and earth started where the tractor opening ended in alders and carried to a large white pine tree perched on the other bank, shading the old cartway.

The dam was wide enough for a dog and hunter to walk across with dry feet and, if the mallard ducks were flying, to lean against and wait for the return of the early-morning puddlers. When the sun was up and the ducks had flown off, I would switch the heavy waterfowl gun for the upland 20-gauge and walk across to the rise of the green hill. The gravel next to the big pine had been pulled down into the stream's road bed, creating a mild incline rising into a mature oak forest.

There were never grouse in the oak woodlot, just the remnants of a logging shelter pulled to the spot and left as a tar-paper shack on sled runners. In those years I hunted with a small, white English setter named Salty and her steady companion, a black Labrador retriever named Dixie. With two dogs, seasoned and experienced and chafing from the inactivity of duck waiting, I lost little time exploring the sparse understory of the oak woods. We always headed east to the other side of the green hill.

The memory of discovering this place is undiminished by time. I had seen, from the Maple Hill churchyard, a green pasture created in a long straight line, like the edge of an alpine meadow on the face of the green hill. Then, inexplicably, it seemed to turn uphill, with stripes of green trees carrying across and filling a square.

"Windrows," I said aloud. "And right between two patches of woods." It looked very birdy even at the distance of a mile. Grouse love edges, and old windrows are edges and edges, one after the other.

"If I walk due east from the Pedersen farm pond, across the state land, to the top of that hill, I should come out on the corner of that first row," I said aloud.

I was very well blessed by my long friendship with the Pedersen farm. I knew every corner and could draw its contours by memory. I was less well acquainted with the hills and woods between the farm and the church.

The traces of the old town road were nothing more than a skylit hallway, but there were enough clues on the floor of the open hardwoods. As I had anticipated, we arrived at the corner of some old bulldozing rows. Seven lines of mixed poplar and birch stretched north and south like terraces along the brow of the hill. Tall grass had grown between them, and gray dogwood bushes had flourished.

I called the dogs back. They were no longer bored. This was bird country. At the foot of the hill was a farm. I could see long, brushy fence lines, with cornfields on either side, and a lap-sided frame house with dairy barns and machine sheds all set above it on the hill. If I had held that mental picture and closed my eyes, it could have been Missouri, and if it had been, the quail hunting would have been fabulous.

I turned to the dogs and pointed toward the buildings. "That is Bob Kangas's farm, girls; we are going to walk down to the pasture, across it, and up to the house. On the way down you are free to explore." If they didn't flush any grouse, I intended to climb back up and return the way I had come. If the grouse were there, I had plenty of time to get permission, then return to hunt them.

Salty had Missouri quail-dog bloodlines. She burst away in a long cast, carrying leaves in her wake and splitting the grass like a torpedo boat. Dixie was content to work the edge of the square as I walked down the bulldozed trail. I know my instincts and, in response, drew both shells out of the barrels. It was a good thing. Dixie made three flushes on just the one side, and Salty had five points, producing seven grouse. It would have been an easy three taken, perhaps more, but not without a penalty. I know this landowner to be generous with those who show him respect, less so with those who don't.

I like to spend some time talking to Bob. Most often, in those early years, he could be found in his dairy barn. Bob always made do with what he had. The barn, like any good farm implement, had been altered where needed. The dairy stalls were clean and simple, and he had a pipeline system. But these pipes were suspended on a log-rafter ceiling. Bob focused on the end product, good clean milk, and was not hung up on what fancier dairies would call "appearances."

After pleasantries and inquires about one another's health and families, I asked his permission for the new parcel. He said yes and went on to explain the hapless plight of two young bear hunters who had killed a large bear, without his permission, not far from the place I was talking about. What they wanted was some farmer to haul the bear out for them. When they explained where the bear was lying, the trespassers discovered that point where sport ends and work begins. Bob emphasized that the direction they wanted him to drag the carcass for them and the direction they were *going* to drag the carcass—by themselves—was off his land and back across the half mile of hard walking they had covered to trespass on his property.

I left the farmyard by climbing through the pasture fence, and instead of heading immediately uphill and into my new bird heaven, I walked out into the cut cornfield to get a view of the whole piece of grouse country I had just lucked into. I faced south, looking down the valley between the green hill on my right and Maple Hill on my left. The center of it was a long swamp of low brush and tall yellow grass. On the right I confirmed the presence of the windrow opening. On the left, there was a lowland hardwood grove. It was a grouse haven by design, with a border of poplar regrowth as a bonus, joined to a wooded pasture. I almost cheered.

The first order of business was to walk straight to the center lowland. Some of this kind of terrain consists of creek bottoms, If so, there is often a series of beaver dams providing sidewalks across the valley from one cover to the next. The dogs led and I followed, boring ahead on high spirits. A new territory ripe with promise and sealed from access on all sides.

Access, on the other hand, does not mean accessible. The remains of an old beaver dam did lie across the swamp but surfaced out in the grass, about a quarter of a mile away. The cornfield I stood in was, in essence, the "lake shore" of a now silted-in pond. All that is grass is not necessarily dry, especially when the "soil" is still sparkling. I had to work my way to the right, back in the direction that I had come. The edge became heavy alder, the old kind. The kind where some limbs lie on the ground but there is still plenty of wood standing upright. Enough bars to prevent any real entry and enough rollers on the earth to keep everything unbalanced.

I suppose everything is traceable to an insignificant source. Somewhere there is a meteorologist who postulates that hurricanes are caused by the air disturbance of a butterfly's wing off the west coast of Africa. So, the sight of a clump of golden grass led to the sight of another, and before long I was crunching old beaver cuttings under my boot soles, believing that this was the way to El Dorado, or perhaps a land bridge to Asia. Either way, it became the source of one more small beginning. The ducks that I had waited for on the Pedersen side of the green hill had spent their day in a pond over here.

But there was no obvious pond. Just more grass, stretching ever outward and down the valley. There were no ducks and then, suddenly, there were ducks enough to sell, to rent, to give away to the poor. Mallards streamed by from right to left, a minor migration in those days. These were also the days before steel shot. The time that passed between my thinking about shooting and the shot was not spent digging the lead loads out of the 20-gauge double in my hands and replacing those with steel. Still, before the little light came on, a lot of ducks went by because a 20-gauge with grouse loads is not the pure death choice for mallard shooting. I was pondering whether a shot, in these circumstances, was a good thing given the size of the ducks, and the size of the gun.

Then, one duck made some sort of a connection with that unknown nerve bundle in the back of my brain stem.

Suddenly it was done. The mallard flew by, hard driving from the right, and the circuit closed. I picked up its flight line with my lead hand, and when the stock hit my cheek the gun went off. It was one of the deadest in-flight ducks I have ever shot. It fell like a hawk diving into a wheat field.

"Oh, man . . . that was . . . dumb." I looked around for my black Labrador. The white setter was content to sit back on the first grass hump. Old Dixie was gone. In my own defense for having taken such a risky shot, Dixie was a superb marking dog. To my own condemnation I honestly did not know if she was around when the world became ducks, therefore I didn't know if she had seen anything.

Of course she had. She saw everything, and limp in her mouth was a fine, plump mallard. This gave me two things to do. Pat her on the head and mark down, mentally, that while this place might be the beginning of Mayo Creek, the green hill side belonged to my old world and the other side would be the new. And the twain would not meet.

CHAPTER THREE
The Trip Wire

The other side, my new world across Mayo Creek, has, of course, been settled by industrious Finns and Norwegians for more than a hundred years. Two things stand as proof of this. Roads are the first, and then there are the wire fences.

A proper fence is carefully defined in township law. It is four strands of wire on a four-foot wooden or steel post. The thing not so well defined is what happens when wire heads off into the woods pulled by two not-so-reliable Norwegians, probably ancestors of mine, and is stapled into place where the "posts" are handy. These posts, however, have leaves and are convenient, if not so evenly spaced.

Four wires become one or two, and a tree becomes a post if it is in more or less the right direction. This creates the kind of fence that is often the subject of a boundary-line dispute. Then the old fence wire becomes a troublesome thing. Unless it is rolled up whenever the fence is rebuilt, it gets mixed up in the grass and turns a dull, rusty brown. As an attorney, I have resurrected many of these fences over the years, and inevitably the trial-court judge has to divine the "intent" of the builders. Since my feet have a talent for finding the hidden loops, I have the answer. I can't win a trial with it, but I know beyond a reasonable doubt that the wire is not there to mark a boundary; it is there to trip an unwary bird hunter.

The fall is not graceful. It is sudden and violent, a sweeping experience. Often leaving a red welt about shin height, the tumble scatters shotshells here and there, and because both hands are saving the gun, the spectacles fly off. The pair of glasses lands in the yellow leaves and slides under the litter. A person as nearsighted as I am must crawl around, stopping to massage the grass and squint between the brush stems for the metallic flash of a brass frame. This exercise is marked by cursing, crawling, and squeezing, all to the ghostly laughter of two long-dead Norwegian fence men who wink at one another and say, "Yah, dat looks 'bout right."

That experience, repeated on more than one occasion, created the name I gave the cover. I call it the Trip Wire.

The Trip Wire is part private and part public. Next to Mayo Creek, between the sparkling swamp grass and the wooded edge of Bob's pasture, wild and lush, is the property of the sovereign County of Cass. The land department of Cass County, unlike the aged members of the Pedersen family, has lots of money for timber management. Bob allowed the county access through two gates in his cow pasture to clear-cut the Trip

Wire's patch of old-growth hardwood.

The new growth that followed provided the shelter and food vital to young grouse broods, and at the same time, the lowland hardwoods gave the parent birds a place to get away from the kids. When the broods split up, the young birds often found their way to another water source. It became an unexpected surprise in golf-course-type surroundings.

One year, Bob dug his cattle a pond in an alder grove along the highway. By stirring around in the thicket, he caused the young sprouts to regenerate. From across the pasture and along Mayo Creek the grouse began to arrive, leaving the loafing ground of their poplar regrowth for the pond thicket by the highway.

I didn't know this until the dog got away.

As I drove onto Bob's farm that day, the first gate led into a muddy cattle-feeding area, so I went on through. The second gate framed a trail that led away so perfectly that the urge to push toward the lush edge of the Mayo was, and remains, irresistible. Fortunately for me, I accidentally left the door open on my old car when I walked back to close the second gate. Having a keen eye for birdy ground, and thinking it was time to hunt, Salty jumped out. The only thing to do was to follow with vest and gun. I learned long ago that shouting and whistling in grouse country gives the birds another reason to run.

The corner was trashy young trees, bunches of gray dogwood, and a low run of alder—good looking enough that I dropped two shells into the Parker double and picked up my pace. Salty was running without her bell (I had that in my left hand), so I couldn't hear where she was. The result was subtle. Since I was now belled, the dog—and the grouse—could hear me coming. I was clueless as to the location of either one of them. At least I was until a bird whizzed past my left ear. That stopped me.

"Salty!" I called in a hoarse off-stage whisper. I have no idea what exactly I expected her to do.

"Salty!" Nothing, not even the sound of feet scuffling in dry leaves, gave me a hint of where to turn. I trotted along the alder run, her bell dinging in my left hand.

"*Whirr-r-r!*" A second grouse got up behind me. I had no chance without the dog. "Salty!" I snapped, a little louder this time but with no return of dog or any movement.

I shook the bell like a Salvation Army Santa. Something white made a small movement behind a clump of brush.

"Ha!" I said. "Lying low to stay out of trouble!" I walked over to the dog in long, fast strides. "I've got you now!"

Salty did hunker down a bit as I *"ding, dinged"* close enough to see that she was otherwise frozen in her tracks.

On point, my eyes said.

Too late! my brain said.

Good-bye, two grouse said as they burst away through the alder tops.

Idiot, Salty said, and that was exactly what I expected.

I have extracted my revenge in the years since then, for now it is my custom to stop immediately after the second gate and to hunt the pasture and its alder corner. The process is a simple matter. I hold the dog in close until we reach the clear spot on the alder edge, about midway, then turn the dog loose with its bell ringing merrily. The grouse in these alders are jumpy and fly more than they hold point. It provides a wonderful chance for a wide-open pass shot and a short, productive hunt.

One early-season afternoon, my son Max—then only six or seven years old—and I followed my usual path. Max was bright in his hooded sweatshirt and glad for the chance to be with the big guys on a real hunt. I had intended a short trip, and it worked out well for me. Salty put up a grouse, it flew true to form, and I dropped it.

"Here," I said to Max, taking the bird from the dog, "put this in your pocket." He took the soft, warm mix of brown and black feathers and stroked it smooth.

"Where's Mike?"

Our companion that afternoon was my old friend Mike McIntosh, here on the first afternoon of our annual grouse hunt, now into its twentieth year and counting.

Max pointed toward the pond part of the alder thicket.

"Well, I wonder what he's doing in there." I said. Little Max shrugged his shoulders and started to walk in that direction. The early fall rain had put the pond and alders into full flood. Mike had probably stepped off to the right as I walked up to the tree line. The place was not familiar to him and he commonly took a place to my right side.

"No matter; come and sit down. He'll be along in a minute," I said and dug in my vest pocket for pipe and matches.

It takes about ten minutes to draw a bowl of fresh tobacco down halfway. Considering that on this occasion the tobacco had been in my hunting vest for a week or two and that the pipe was a 1935 Hardcastle of my father's, caked and cracked, I would estimate that Mike was missing for around fifteen minutes. I didn't want to spoil his chances, so I did not call out. As I said, the birds in this alder run are jumpy.

I saw Mike's dog first. It was wet from nose to tail. Then I saw Mike. He looked as if he had been seized, body and soul, by a baptizing wild man who had doused him in the Mayo.

There is a moment that passes between men when they are at a loss for words. It is not an empty moment; rather, it is just a space, an opening like the few inches in front of a charging bull.

Mike closed the distance between us in that pregnant moment and stood quite still. The water dripped from the pockets of his game vest, pattering onto the leaves. "Lord," he said, "thy sea is so large, and my boat is so small," and we both laughed. He had turned the wrong way at my shot and had pressed on through a wall of alder saplings and waist-high flooded swamp grass until he stepped into the open air above Mayo Brook.

"Michael," I said, "a man once was asked: 'Do you believe in baptism?' His answer was 'Hell yes, I've seen it done!' Well, Mike," I said reprising my best revival-minister's accent, "Now I believe!"

Mike's answer was "I would have preferred a laying-on of the hands."

Miracles do happen in the Trip Wire.

The wet world that so suddenly doused Mike was no accident. The beavers had built a dam almost at the same place where the pasture fence meets the water but a quarter-mile from the cornfield. It was the first dam I had walked on when I tried to come in from the green hill side. It did not span the creek, or its swamp, but rather was a small pile, not anywhere near the class of engineering represented by the dam that was constructed on the Wood Row Creek side of the green hill.

Seen from the sky, the Mayo Creek valley would be a straight line of trees along the pasture side, a low grassy slough comprising two or three ponds within the brook, and mature hardwoods on the slope of the green hill. In the middle, between the straight line of trees and the pasture is a large clear-cut, now in the process of regrowing its poplar. All along the swamp of the brook, where the trees still stand, is a border of sparkling, coffee-colored holes; fallen limbs; and soft ground, preventing any land walking creature from crossing to the other side.

Who would have thought that there could be a grouse in the thin margin where the cornfield, pasture, and wet swamp edge met? But, there it was, and behind it was my dog, Beans, frozen in midstride by the sight of a bird so utterly naked. Max was to my right, only ten feet away. The point, the collective amazement, and the flush happened about as fast as you read it here.

The grouse came up off the grass, climbing into the few limbs that were between us and turning toward the open pasture behind. I had one clear moment to sweep the barrel past the tail, across its head, and slap the trigger. The bird dropped a leg but continued to pour its strength into a long climb that started fast, then slowed like a plane running out of gas. On and on it climbed, trying to reach that one last note of its crescendo. The flight peaked, and the grouse began a glide toward a small pine woodlot, the tops of which I could see almost four hundred yards away.

"Watch it, watch this one closely, Max. It's going to collapse," I said. But it didn't. The bird cupped its wings and disappeared against the trees.

I turned to Max and started to say that I was going to walk over to the grove when I caught sight of a grouse coming from that direction. It was headed straight for us in a fixed-wing glide. The bird swept in between Max and me, bouncing once on the grass, then bouncing a second time, and skidding to a halt, stone dead.

It landed within three feet of where it took off.

"Do you think it's the same one?" asked Max.

"Well, unless another grouse was flying by and died of a heart attack, I think it has to be."

*   *   *

A small three-leaved plant grows in that part of the Trip Wire lying between the clear-cut and the brook seepage. It loves the low, lush, wet ground between trees, remaining a bright green carpet for a long time after all else is lost to the frost. If the crop of the first day's bird shows this plant, other plans can be abandoned. It is in this place and others like it that the grouse will be found. As the mayfly is to trout, the little fern-like foliage is to the grouse. Because of it, the birds are drawn to test their fates in this alley. A botanist could identify the plant; I can't. Nor do I care how it fits into the scheme of nature's tapestry, except during a few damp days in October.

The tall hardwoods of the low ground, spread in a narrow band along the side of the Mayo seepage, can be a chaos of shooting, flying, and retrieving. The level of intensity becomes both delicious and dangerous, for grouse are diving, turning, and escaping two or three at a time. Points become downhill flushes as the birds try to get out into the creek alders. It takes a cool head and steady nerves to mark the downed birds, call the flushing grouse, and keep track of where everybody is. As the hunters move through the corridor, the birds that don't break off into the creek bottom start to pile up in a tangle of poplar, downed logs, and heavy brush at the end, where the clear-cut comes down to meet the edge of the narrow woods.

It is here that a pile of tree trunks and debris was once pushed up into a knot of twisted wood. This is where the fugitives want to stop. I was alone the first year that I sat there to rest, in the hope of catching my breath. One of the dogs came down from the dense regrowth and clambered up onto some of the larger logs. In the next two or three seconds I counted a dozen—twelve different individuals—that flushed from around me. I recovered my wits in time to kill one.

The birds spread out from there. The woods get bigger, and the space is larger because the Mayo bends away, leaving more room for the woods to grow trees. There is room, too, for men, birds, and dogs. But before this gathering point, about midway in the shooting ground of tall trees, there is a sofa. It is at that point where a bird hunter's senses are keyed to the breaking point. Stuck almost fifteen feet up the trunk of an ash tree is a full-size, brown plaid sofa with its back wedged against the trunk. Held up by two wide-spaced limbs underneath, it is the penultimate of deer stands.

It is also the benchmark, the icon, for a necessary piece of advice: It is time to slow down. If you don't relax and take a break, the pace here could kill you—or your hunting partner. The emotion of excitement is good because it sharpens the eyes and quickens the instincts. It is bad because it accumulates like good liquor, clouding judgment and dulling restraint. Excitement is contagious and passes among hunting partners, first charging one, then the other. The chase becomes the thing to seek—until it bursts, and that which was the predator becomes the prey.

Bob White

CHAPTER FOUR
Pursuit

Everything we remember seems to happen to music. I guess that is why movies have it in the background. It would be a nice thing in the real world, sometimes. Just before a man got himself into a dangerous corner, he could be forewarned by those tension-building notes. I always seem to have a tune running around in my mind as I pick through my grouse covers.

I used to hum a few bars about "second chances." Then I switched tunes because I was missing too many birds and figured the song was unlucky. I followed that music with several notes and words concerning the pride of some Texas backfield. The problem there was that the tune was catchy, and I would stop every now and then and dance a little.

Take my advice on this one: Stick to music that has lots of harmony, and if you ever meet your mirror image, don't try to out-pick him and don't take him grouse hunting. It becomes dueling banjos.

In his essay "When a Man's thoughts are Pure," Havilah Babcock wrote:

> *"I want a companion to be friendly, but not too friendly; to be talkative, but not too talkative; to have a good dog, but not quite as good as mine; to have a sense of humor without being a humorist. . . . I also want a companion who is a good shot, but not too damned good."*

At best, my father was a middling wingshot and a part-time hunter. He started this whole bird-hunting life of mine without so much as a shove. Within three years of my first shotgun, Dad hurt his back and never went out again. He didn't have to. My brother and I had our own shotguns, driver's licenses, and—most importantly—the keys to the old Jeep. From sunrise to dusk that wheezy old gas seeper boiled itself over on grouse trails, bogs, frozen lakes, and streams. From September to December, as he viewed his two sons, Dad must have thought, "What have I started, and where did this come from?" Even if he had wanted to go along, there was no room left for him to hunt birds. I occupied all the space that nature allowed. All the chairs in the bird-hunting orchestra were filled.

Over the years, my hunting companions have always measured up to Havilah Babcock's rule. They occupied different chairs in the orchestra. My son, Max, has no middling bird hunter to be better than. Try as I may, I cannot turn down the juice. I have resolved, mightily, to lower the heat of my fire when he is with me. It works, for a while, but if the birds are flying and the action is fast—or frustrating—the lead musician must lead. Max wants to prove that he can keep the pace. He has an ear for the music, but his skills are wanting. When I am older and slower, he will surge past. But this was not to be on the day when Dale came, and the background music became dueling banjos.

Dale is an irreducible element. It's a fact that salt and water mix. But don't take the same sodium and eliminate the calcium. Because sodium and water make fire. It's just too much of two good things. Mike McIntosh had invited him to come along to our grouse hunt that year, and, Mike might have been the calcium that united our two elements. Fate and publisher's deadlines, however, pushed Mike away from the scheduled week. Dale and I had never hunted together.

We knew after the first day, in the way that two top seed pointers know, that we were the same. We knew there was no room in the stew for so much salt. Behind us, in the vacuum, being sucked up like leaves after a fast dog's charge, was Max.

Two old hunting dogs do a lot of circling and smelling. They get it figured out. It's about the birds. Two humans spend a lot of time being polite and never get it figured out. The Mayo Creek may have been named after two humanitarians, but it is still water, and Dale and I were still smoldering blocks of sodium with no calcium to cool us. A bad place for so much horsepower.

The brush still had about half its leaves, making a texture of screened openings. The land came up, slowly, from the creek valley, but no one could feel this with their feet. The dog—trusting, faithful, and hot running—was not down low but rather about head high, behind the foliage, searching, pointing, and then flushing the grouse, one at a time. Flushing them high enough to be seen, but never in the clear.

That country fiddle player may have said that the devil went down to Georgia, but on that day he was picking the high notes in Minnesota on two tightly strung banjos, because our first touch with Mayo Creek's Trip Wire covey was explosive.

We formed a three-man line in low ground where the tree trunks are scattered on top of coffee-colored water holes. Max was in the middle; Dale and I on each side. In between the trees, the sunlight filtered yellow through the hardwood canopy. I had killed the first grouse. Then my shorthair, Beans, pointed in front of Max, I could see it all from my place halfway up the hill. I was feeling pleased with myself, one bird ahead of my guest. I gestured to Max, impatiently, "Walk in, walk in." He did, and at the same instant a grouse flushed—and died—in front of Dale. His kill flushed the pointed birds, giving Max a two-shot chance, but no birds fell.

"They're spreading out ahead of us," I yelled, "at least five, maybe more."

It was more. Another flushed—and died—in front of Dale.

Two more flew away from Max, saluted, but remained untouched.

Beans picked up speed. There was lots of bird scent to follow, and he was happy. Pointing and moving, Beans drew us along at a pace just faster than a brisk walk. A couple of wild flushes turned my head away from my companions walking below. There were grouse everywhere, yet I was frustrated with no chance for a shot. Not a good situation for a fast mover like me.

Beans was somewhere on point. Dale shot again, taking his third.

"The guy is a grouse magnet," I thought.

Max fired twice more, to no effect.

"This isn't a grouse hunt," I thought, "it's a coon hunt—jumping over trees, dodging around bushes, chasing the hounds."

Max fired again. Then there were two more shots, almost simultaneous. Dale had his fourth.

"Max, did you hit anything?" I called.

"No." He answered.

"Where's the dog?" I yelled.

"Over here!" The answer came from Dale's direction.

Here's where a little background music would have helped. I had the lyrics: Damn dog has abandoned me, kid can't hit his hat, and I have yet to fire a second shot. Do you remember that little banjo riff after the first five notes of "Dueling Banjos" in the movie *Deliverance*?

The lesser gods leave signs for their errant children. Before me appeared the tall oak where the sofa was perched.

"Time out," it said. "Kick back, slow down, tempo allegro, not crescendo."

But, the bugle was blown, and I, first chair to no one else, would not be cooled. As if to confirm my role, a grouse flew past

Dale . . . one shot . . . and Max . . . a second shot . . . before it fell to my gun.

"Hah, wiped both their eyes."

And the killing ground slowly raised.

The swamp fell away to the right, and we could see each other, sometimes, between the trees. A grouse flushed wild in front of Max. He swung his gun up lightning fast, shot, and it tumbled! A second movement caught my eye beyond Max. Dale was lowering his gun. Had they shot simultaneously?

"I got one!" yelled Max.

Damn! I wanted my son to kill a bird. I don't know whether he wanted to or not, but I didn't care. Anger surged up, and I put my hand up to my mouth and bit down on my glove. I don't hide my emotions well, and I didn't want Max's moment to be soured.

Beans appeared out of the thick brush in front of us carrying the grouse. I took it from him and brought it to Max.

"Good shot, all instinct, just the way it should be," I said.

Dale stepped around a bush, carrying his own bird. They had each shot one!

I was behind! Damn the naysayers. Full speed ahead!

And the killing ground slowly raised.

Just at the edge of the big woods, the sunlight grows the hazel brush thick and heavy. It prospers in clumps, head high, and beyond it, at the edge of the town road, a line of trees marks the ditch. The next grouse, running and dodging ahead of the dog, had lost the race. The only way out for it was to fly, over the clump of hazel and uphill to the far tree line. But Beans is a cagey grouse hunter. He was not behind this bird, as before; he was coming toward his hunters and right at the hiding place. Now the grouse could see a human from one side and a dog from the other. He panicked and flew directly into an leaf-screened opening, directly over the dog.

A boy, primed and pumped, will shoot quickly and instinctively, as instructed. The load will spread out, uncaring and unreturnable, a sizzling buzz saw.

On the battlefield, when a shell fragment strikes an arm or a leg, it hits with a fine hardness, like getting slapped with the end of a belt. The blood runs free and red, until it cools, and it makes your pant leg sticky. You are not really aware of it. It makes you yell and hop. I heard Beans scream like that.

The same fragment, going deep into a body, drops a man. *Thud.* You can hear it. Just like that. I know, for I was once a soldier.

Beans cried out, and ran to me, the source of all good things, streaming blood. His eyes were clear and open, confused about it all but not pierced. No bubbles or pink froth came from his nose or mouth. Both ears had bleeding holes, one pellet had raked the top of his head. There were two hits in the front of one shoulder and one on the other. I folded my bandanna and pressed it on the shoulder wounds. The bleeding started to quit almost immediately. A river of blood ran from the dog's ear leathers, making the whole scene grisly as a slaughterhouse.

Max was standing close by, clutching his gun to his chest and shaking with sobs.

"Oh God, oh God, I am so sorry," he sobbed and sobbed.

"Max," I said. He sat down, putting his head on his knees and shaking.

Dale sat nearby praying softly.

The dog was about to be the least wounded of us all.

"Max!" I repeated, more emphatically.

He looked at me. "Come here, I need your help." I had to get him involved or lose him to this memory forever.

"Do you have a handkerchief?" I asked.

"Yes," he said. He took it out of his pocket.

"Put it right here," I said pressing the cloth on Beans's ear.

"He's going to be fine, son. We'll just rest here for a bit. How are you?"

"Scared. I didn't mean it. I didn't see him." He started to cry again.

"Max, it's okay. It was my fault." I said.

"Your fault? You didn't shoot him!"

"I didn't pull the trigger, but I could have prevented it," I answered.

"How?"

"I'll explain later. In the meantime, let's see if he can walk."

The shock was wearing off, and though each step was wobbly, stiff, and thoroughly defeated, both Max and Beans walked back to the truck, side by side.

They had ended up as the main chorus of this devil's song.

While there are no hard, fast, and written rules of conduct, outside of how often death can be administered, the ingredients in the witch's brew of this day were foreseeable. I failed to act. I should have sat down and declared an eight bar rest. Instead, I pounded on my drum, responding to the rhythm of Dale's. Two lead dogs on the hot scent of prey, each with one eye on the trail and one on each other. Behind us, caught in the seat of the runaway bandwagon, were Max and Beans, trying to catch up to a fast-marching band.

In my heedless pursuit to finish first, I forgot to listen to some quieter sounds, and at the cymbal crash of Max's gun, the orchestra piled up, and the bandstand collapsed.

As Havilah Babcock said, you can only do one thing with a dead bird—eat it.

I could have done only one thing with my dead dog—bury it. I was lucky, because into that grave would have gone all the beauty and joy of a boy's pursuit of game, both in obedience to my will.

Maybe the old man wasn't so middling after all.

Bob White

CHAPTER FIVE
An Educated Grouse

It all started with education. I was in the second grade. Mrs. Flategraff put me in charge of the Thanksgiving paper-cutout display.

It was going to be the best ever, complete with white-collared pilgrims, colorful turkeys, and Indians in war paint. (This seems to be a conflict of terms, but I was seeking color here.) The class was busy until they all left for recess. All except for me. I was caught up in the pageant, and I was not alone. There was one other student in the classroom. Geraldine, of the long, dark hair and deep brown eyes.

I was caught all right. Even a seven year old can fall under the spell of thick raven locks and brown-eyed adoration. Paper, paste, and scissors; white pilgrim collars; and a quiet touch on my arm:

"Ted, whatever you do will be the best."

I still remember Geraldine.

I am now standing before the house on the farm where she grew up. It has been abandoned for years, and half the porch floor sags under even the light weight of rotted boards. The farm borders the north Mayo Creek watershed, with lots of little veins—capillaries really—feeding the channel into its inconspicuous beginning. It is a black mud basin just over the hill.

The owner before the current one was a computer engineer from Virginia. He bought it, grown over in weeds and rank grass, from a land speculator. I wrote him a letter asking permission for bird hunting and in response received the courtesy and a small bit of history. The premises was used only in the summer, and then just for two weeks. "A wooden tent," he called it.

The engineer had the farm's poplar clear-cut, which in turn had attracted my attention and the attention of two or three grouse coveys. (Not that a grouse's attention has any great span.)

Consider, if you will, the relative size of the grouse brain in comparison to man's. The bird brain is hardly a thousandth in weight, energy, and intellect. Just a few simple synapses to run basic functions of sight, flight, and survival. Hardly more than a bright little light between its brown eyes.

On the other hand, consider the mind of the Almighty in comparison to man's. If God's eye, as Ethel Waters sings, is on even the lowly sparrow, then He must watch the grouse with at least equal interest. If so, the antics of grouse hunters like me must provide countless opportunities for celestial amusement.

Does God have a sense of humor? No doubt about it. Consider the woodcock. I don't know on what day He created this species, but I do know that all he had on hand was spare parts, and he got the brain in upside down. This is a joke He can share with us. We can laugh together.

The grouse is God's joke on the bird hunter. It is God's extension of fly-by-wire from heaven to earth. If He is in a mind to brim His eyes with tears of laughter, then He comes to earth in a grouse cover, puts on His goggles and a silk scarf, and lights up the birds' little brains. It is all about education.

I remember when Beans, the German shorthair, was just a little over a year old. He was big, bony, and fast. The old setter, Salty, was still alive that year, and I hunted the two of them together until I thought Beans had a feeling for the range of grouse hunting.

On our first afternoon without the old dog, the hunt went badly. My "Geraldine" had a two-rut, grass-center tote road running down the middle. We had just reached the first turn when a grouse flushed wild from the roadside, banking to the right and cutting back over the dog's head. Beans pursued.

I whistled him back, took him to the place where the bird had flushed, and made him stand firm. So it went for a quarter of a mile, then a quarter more. He was too pumped up. The late, cool afternoon air and a slight north breeze all combined to turn bird scent into liquor. The young turk was drunk.

I gave it up. On the way back Beans ran far ahead, casting left and right, until he was around the corner. When I got there he was gone. I saw the white flag of a deer in the far edge of a hardwood grove.

"Oh, oh."

I blew on the whistle and blew again. Back and forth on the trail I walked, blowing the whistle and calling, on and on until full dark. The only return was the barking of a farm dog, a mile away.

My boy was gone.

I have been really scared a few times in my life. It is always the same. The feeling rises from the middle and climbs in a river of prickles, almost like living radio static, up under the chin and then out across the cheekbones. The real thing. Life without a movie ending.

There was nothing left to do. I walked back to the truck. I had parked at the old farmhouse, so I sat at the porch for a while.

Beans's blanket was in the back of the vehicle. I left it and some food in a bowl right alongside the steps. If he followed my tracks back to this spot, perhaps he, too, would be home bound by the dark-haired and brown-eyed spirit of this sad place.

It was a restless night. I was up at 2 A.M. and again at 4 A.M. Sunrise would not come by my willing it. At 6 A.M. I was in the truck and on the road, afraid to hope for a happy ending. I turned onto the trail and pulled into the overgrown farmyard. The old house, peeled and brown, stood looking at me with dark, deep windows.

A gray face with sad brown eyes peered out from under the steps.

"Beans!"

I was out of the truck and he was leaping into my arms. It was the end of his ranging days. It's all about education. He had been educated, and God had not been joking.

Geraldine got sold again. The old house was crushed up and buried. A new, modern home was built and marked for resale.

It looked like the end for Geraldine, but remember: God has a sense of humor.

The field next door belonged to Bob Kangas, and I had permission to hunt there. The first full forty acres, from the road heading east, was one-half alfalfa; the rest was standing corn. The next forty acres was partially wooded along the fence it shared with Geraldine. Better yet, the woods ran alongside my old cover to its junction with the state land. I still had at least half of a good thing. My education was about to begin.

The first principle in the lesson book is: "Look, but don't touch."

Bob's woods were mature maple. Lovely to walk in, a picture of fall scarlet and yellow, the woodlot offered me only a tantalizing panorama of Geraldine's old, forbidden, and tempting contours. Oh, once she was mine! On my side of the fence was the kind of scene outdoor artists like to paint. Full-page grouse flying through open mature trees. On the other side, in Geraldine's arms, was the real thing.

She had it all. Firm young poplar, smooth-skinned and lush, backed up against the full, round edges of mature growth. She had the heavy fruits where she needed them and soft moist clearings where those left off. One hundred twenty beautiful acres sculpted to bird-heaven perfection. I should know. She once was mine, but now she was gone. The grouse in there would die of old age and high living.

The next educational principle is: "Pretty girls have ugly sisters."

It all comes, I guess, from one beauty using up all the gene pool. Geraldine was surrounded by state land. Bitter to the bone, it had been forfeited for taxes years before because the owners died of abuse and hard luck. Those parts with trees grew them in the muddy pool of North Mayo's humble beginnings. Hummocks surrounded by hard black brush and itch weed. The gray dogwood on the few edges that got sunlight had small, hard, fuzzy green berries and not many of those. Even worse, the stumps and limbs lying on the ground were sharp-tongued and stabbed readily. Shins, legs, and more private parts got stuck in twisted, knotty, weed-covered ambushes. If there was a grouse hunters' therapy group for that piece of ground, its mantra would have been "God knows I tried!"

Of course He knew, because the last principle was "God loves the long drop."

The long drop is that space between the story and the punch line, and God uses the grouse for a straight man.

There is an island of cover, hanging on the edge of the maple woods like the leaf on a red apple. It is surrounded by standing corn. I don't know how I could have missed it before, but sweat makes my eyes burn and an afternoon spent in the ugly sister surrounding my beautiful Geraldine narrows a bird hunter's focus. Nevertheless, I saw it that day.

I called Beans over for a conference. "See that bunch of trees over there? No, not that one, the other one, sticking out into the cornfield." He looked up at me. I pointed with the little 20-gauge double. "That little island with the rocks piled along the edge. We are going to go over there and poke through it."

The dog didn't seem all that eager to go. I put it off to a negative attitude gained by his innate German pessimism. But that wasn't the reason. Beans has good ears; he could hear snickering. He had been listening to it all afternoon.

My hearing is just barely adequate. I have a permanent chorus of crickets in my head. Some of it was lost by close association to gun noises, but most of my deafness is induced by education. I don't hear sounds because my mind has excluded them. Birds don't talk, trees can't whisper, and the only sound of any consequence is the human voice.

Beans is one of the lesser gods. He hears the rest of the world. God speaks to bird dogs in the rustle of leaves under the pads of their feet, in the thin smoke of bird scent, and in a hundred other languages that man once knew but forgot how to hear. He knew, before we crossed the open hay field, that there were grouse on the island and that they were wired for divine guidance.

The closer I got, the better it looked. Gray dogwood bushes, lush with berries, stood in a dense cuff around the poplar trees. It was almost possible to see through the grove from one side to the other. Standing corn on three sides and on the base, an overgrown trail separating the island from the maple mainland. Any bird caught feeding along those corn-rimmed shores was going to be a cinch to point and shoot.

I would play the habits against the species. Grouse don't like to fly into the open. They are not pheasants; therefore, the corn will hold them inside the trees. The understory was open, shaded into short grass by the dogwood leaves. Every opportunity would be a good one.

Beans reached the first clump of bushes and raised his head abruptly. He had heard something. It turned out to be a guffaw, audible to him as laughter and to me as a roar of wings. Two grouse flushed out of a maple tree, diving to level out a foot or so above the berry tops, then banking sharp left to land on the far side of the woods.

"Hsh! I was right, Beans, we've got them now. Hunt 'em up, boy!"

The dog pointed solidly in a half turn, looking to his right. He had a new one between the bushes and the corn row. I stepped backward, then out and around the brush, walking quickly along the smooth dirt path. The bird should have been between us.

Perhaps, I thought, if I bend over and peer under the stems I can catch a glimpse, maybe the quick jerk of a head will show me where it is. That would have been true if the bird had been under the bushes. This one, however, was out in the corn about three rows.

I have heard grouse in thick brush, in dense leaves, and even in pine branches, but until that moment I had never heard one flush out of field corn.

It sounds a lot like, well, dry laughter.

I asked God to damn the bird and yelled after it that its mother was unmarried.

No matter, I still had two others as good as dead. Beans circled the edge and within fifty yards found the vapor trail. He pointed, let go, pointed again, carefully stepped forward a few steps, and then tilted forward like a swordsman. It was as good as done.

The question was choosing the direction from which to gain the best shot. If I came in from the cornfield, the birds would fly into the trees. On the other hand, if I cut through the trees, I could pin them both against the corn barrier and force the flush up into the clear air. The decision was made.

Quickly, quickly, I reminded myself; grouse won't wait for a dawdler. I got into position and waited. I waited some more. Beans waited. It was taking a lot longer than I thought it should. One of the three of us had to have some relief. I stepped toward the dog . . . and almost on top of the first grouse. It rose, flapping a furious clamor straight up in my face. My first shot was an involuntary jerk up into the sky. The second was better only because I got the gun mounted. It was still a clean miss.

I opened the gun, put my gloved hand over the breech, and caught the empties. We've all done this—you know, formed your hand into a fist and banged it against your forehead. Then, with eyes closed, tilted your head back and hollered at the sky. It usually made Beans drop to his belly and turn his head side to side.

Not this time. He was still on point. He was smart enough to remember that there were two birds, or perhaps he could hear the second one gasping for breath as it held its aching sides. Regardless, I held an empty gun as it walked out, bold as a crow;

looked at me, then the dog; and flushed away. I left the gun open, balanced it on my shoulder, and walked back through the corn and across the green alfalfa to the truck.

Education, the essence that clarifies the difference between two minds. As humans we are bound by our senses. We learn by seeing, hearing, smelling, and feeling. The rest of the natural world is not so constrained. If man can make a seed-sized computer chip containing gigabytes of information, then consider what God has done with a few fundamental bird-brain synapses, a sense of humor, some marginal habitat, and an uneducated grouse hunter.

CHAPTER SIX
Under the Surface of Things

While I don't ordinarily indulge myself in sayings, I couldn't resist this time. The fellow on the other end of the phone was explaining to me the reason why he decided not to buy my client's little store. Never mind that the signed contract said he would. There was a serious problem.

"And that is?" I replied.

"Benzine," he said.

"Explain that, please," I returned.

Taking the tone of a person just barely able to tolerate such pure ignorance, the voice cleared its podium and ascended the pulpit. It was well known to any environmentally sensitive person, it said, that a certain gas station in southern California had been determined to be the source of benzine molecular ground water pollution at a site in Arizona.

"I didn't know that," I said.

The wonderment in my reply was not caused by this startling

disclosure; it was, well, expressed in my next question to him.

"How does that affect this purchase?"

"Hah!" he said with the conviction of a true believer, "I have it on good authority that seven blocks from your client's store there is a gas station with buried fuel tanks. If benzine can pollute a site 700 miles from California, it can pollute the ground under the store."

And so it was that I, in a weakened state, indulged myself, and said:

"You're not from around here, are you?"

This concept of a mighty underground river sucking California dry was worth exploring. "Someone ought to inform the authorities," I offered, hoping to fill the pause that my quip had opened. There was a click on the other end of the line.

A couple of days later, October had arrived in living color, and I was standing at the back door of Gilbert's farmhouse. My wife calls this "neighboring." She has a strong line of farm genetics and has explained to me that nice people in small towns take the time to exchange information ("and don't charge a fee for it!").

Gilbert's little farm is a lovely part of my world. On one side is an eighty-acre woodlot of mixed hardwoods, pastured into brushy clumps of hazel and gray dogwood. In the middle and extending to the south is a wide, wet, grassy swamp. It seeps water from its big footprint into a small drain and eventually finds its way into North Mayo Creek. The house is in the middle, and on the other side the land breaks into long windrows of poplar, intertwined with berry bushes. The rows mark, in quarter-mile borders, the old, rotted-down piles that used to be trees but are now pasture edges, like long hallways with green carpet between them.

The concept of the underground river in California was still in my mind, and I shared some of my astonishment with my host. He failed to be amazed. In fact, he explained that the wet swamp that made up the center of the grouse woods came from an underground flow that started in a certain black-mud slough hole to the north of this place—from the very same place I knew as the ugly sister of my treasured covert Geraldine.

When it came to Mayo Creek, I began to wonder if I was a human witching wand following the invisible attraction of its flow.

Gib doubted that. He had seen a lot of water witchers in his time and said I didn't have the nose for it.

Appearances can be deceiving. For instance, I am the most ordinary-looking fellow you ever saw. At just six feet and a hundred sixty-five pounds, I barely leave a footprint on hard soil. Sporting wire-rimmed glasses and a half-gray mustache on a square Scandinavian face, I might pass as a skinny Theodore Roosevelt.

However, cows look at me and say, "I don't know what it is, but there's just something about you that I hate."

This is a problem because grouse grow in the woods here. In between me and the bird cover is a pasture. And, in the pasture there are cows. Lots of cows, the meanest bunch of ill-mannered mothers on four hooves. It is so bad for me that before I stop to hunt this covert, which I call "Gibby's," I have to drive by and look into the pasture. If the herd is down in the south end or out in the windrows, the coast is clear. If not, I look for another place, or, at least, I used to. Things are better now, for I have an ally.

She is a short, stout cattle dog called a blue heeler. She is my bodyguard. She and I were not always friends. We were, at best, distant acquaintances. I was the guy that came into her yard with my bird dogs—uninteresting, sniffly, meddlesome, German things without a real job and damn little prospect of ever getting one.

Then, at some point, she noticed that the cow herd took an uncommon interest in my demise. There was the time they caught me halfway across the field and gave me a good hard chase back to the house. I had to hurdle the fence and even then was just barely ahead of the snot-blowing leader. Poor old Beans got cut off by the young stock, and they shagged him up one side of the field and down the other until he found a hole in the woven wire and slipped through. Apparently, the noise and turmoil of all that running and chasing was too disorderly for the blue heeler. The herd belonged to her, and they were clearly out of hand.

I don't think she really had any interest in protecting me. I think she was just bent on proving to the cows, and my bird dogs, that this sort of conduct had gone on long enough. The next time I hunted Gib's farm, I parked in the yard, over by the machine shed, and as I pulled on my vest and drew the little 20-gauge out of its case, I could see the cows start to gather along the single strand of electric fence. A gate of one thin strand of wire and 110 volts of household current was all that was holding back several tons of bad temper. Beans and the little cow dog were rubbing noses, and, I had just decided to give it up and move to the next place.

Then the blue heeler left the bird dog and walked over to me. Standing up on her hind legs, she rested her front paws on my pant leg, asking for a scratch between the ears.

What a nice thing, I thought, a stubbed-off, shorthaired, blue and gray spotted artillery shell. But, I like friendly dogs and I loved this farm. Maybe tomorrow, I thought, saying out loud: "I think I'm going to move on, my little teapot; the cattle are in a mood to chase bird hunters."

She dropped back to all fours and shook off my attention. One look into those eyes, and I knew what she was thinking:

"Baloney, nothing out there but hot-dog filling,"

In a charge worthy of a center linebacker, she scattered cow-calf pairs like a shark moving through herring.

"C'mon Beans," I said, "we are in the care of she-who-must-be-obeyed." I picked up a stick and pushed down the electric wire, stepped over it, then pressed the strand down again so that Beans could hop over.

The big, red, walleyed leader cow came around behind us but stopped short. The stout little heeler was lying flat on her belly with her nose between her feet. She had the old cow leveled with a deadly skunk eye. The lead cow stood her ground—and lost the argument as our caretaker charged straight for the big, juicy nose. The herd was in full retreat, and our way into the woods was secured.

We crossed the fence and waited. The little heeler came trotting over, tongue lolling out, laughing in the way that dogs do after a long, happy chase.

"Thanks partner" I said, "you are the expert. Now we can go bird hunting."

"And," she replied as she sat on my boot, "I'm coming along."

You see, working dogs are wage earners. They expect to be paid.

Now, I've hunted with all sorts and varieties of dogs. I spent one afternoon in Missouri hunting quail with a bluetick hound. He adopted me as the next best thing to his lost pack of coon hunters. He had one ice-blue eye and no talent for pointing birds. But he was sure death on rabbits. After he figured out that I wasn't shooting any and that the other dogs were busy with their own business, he left.

A year later, it was a three-legged farm variety of bird dog, with a tail that curled back into a question mark every time he pointed. He was sure death on quail singles and worked them so well and so thoroughly that my little setter gave up and lay down. She knew enough to keep silent in the presence of greatness.

So, while I had my doubts about a bird-hunting cattle herder, I had seen uglier dogs hunt pretty well, I owed her some wages, and a little extra company couldn't hurt. It was, after all, her woods.

Beans set on about his business, circling the brush clumps and checking the berry bushes for grouse scent. My new companion cow dog watched with interest, made some tentative casts, but in general did what we did, hunted steady and hard.

Since the wind was from the south, we turned into it along the bottom of the big swamp. Because the cows often find their way through, or over, the fence separating the woods from the pasture, there are walkable paths between hazel-brush clumps. These islands of leafy buggy whips are perfect for those birds that like to loaf in the sun. I had six productive points. I know this because I could see Beans, staunch as starch, and hear the bird flushing, unseen. The grouse love to run in this part of Gibby's and seldom offer a shot, flushing early and dodging between the leafy tops. If Beans pointed, the cow dog would wait. If I shot— and I did that several times—she would look up at me with the most curious expression.

"The bird cut left," I explained to her, "that bush top covered the turn." Or, "I was above that one; if it had kept climbing I would have had him." Finally, I connected and Beans brought the bird back, all loose jointed and happy. The stout little cow dog walked forward and sniffed the bird in his mouth.

"This is it?" She seemed to say.

"A critic," I replied. "That was as good a shot as any you will ever see. Don't be leaping to judgment, cattle dog; if cows had wings, I'd be shooting them too."

"And missing them, no doubt," she sniffed.

A fence and the neighbor's open-grass pasture run along the south side of the swamp, creating a physical barrier. Posted land is a world apart. Gibby's neighbor was pretty clear in stating his intent that humans were not welcome. "No truspassin," was clearly painted in white on an old tire impaled on a fence post. Beans and I—and the cow dog—stood pensively, like three kids outside the circus fence. Though the land beyond the fence was overgrazed cattle ground, the fence line along our edge was stiff with gray dogwood. Beans searched out a grouse in short order, and it flushed, right to left, out into the clear air above the cow grass. I made a fine shot, possibly the best of the day. The gray-tailed speedster bounced like a feathered ball on the turf and now lay, quite dead, in plain sight.

"No truspassin" repeated the white-lettered tire. Reading, however, is not a skill that dogs possess.

The bottom part of the fence was, like the other parts, woven-lattice sheep wire. I looked at my tall, lanky pointer, then, at the stubby little heeler. They stared back.

"I suppose I could crawl over the fence, walk out, pick up the bird, and then prepare my argument based upon the law of fair chase or hot pursuit," I said.

I sat down on a nearby stump. "That'll work really well with the guy who wrote those words. The warning is right there on the surface of that tire, and ignorance of the law is not an excuse." I stood up, leaning my 20-gauge against the stump and addressing the two dogs.

"Ladies and gentlemen of the jury, ignorance implies a lack of education. In this case the education cannot be imparted, since neither of you speak or read the language." I reached down and grasped the bottom of the woven wire, lifting it high enough to make a low passageway, just right for a short-coupled dog.

She knew what to do and was quickly back in under the wire, dragging the grouse by one wing and parading it in front of Beans.

So it went until we had completed our circle around the big

swamp, collecting one more grouse and a pocket full of empty shotshells. Beans and I stood at the woodlot fence, man and bird dog, faced once again with the squinty stare of the herd. But we were not alone.

"Stand aside, noisy man, it is game time," said the blue gray cannonball, and she streaked out from under the bottom wire.

It is not the size of the dog in the fight, it is the size of the fight in the dog. "Run for your lives!" bellowed the herd, because the teapot cow dog was as game as any contender in the world.

I had waited a long time for this moment. I walked, slowly and arrogantly, across the open grass pasture, as safe as a babe in its mother's arms. The dogs slipped under the single electric wire on the far side of the field, and as I stepped over, my bodyguard trotted back into her little house by the kitchen door and lay down, resting her nose on her front paws.

I slipped my shotgun back into its case. Beans jumped up into the back of the pickup. We were ready to go. I leaned back against the open tailgate and packed my pipe slowly, pushing the loose ribbons of tobacco into the bowl. Appearances are deceiving, I thought. What seems to be dry land is just a sieve for an underground river. I've had distinguished-looking gentlemen lie to my face and seen Cadillac-driving paupers. But I never thought I'd see a bird-hunting cow dog, and I never thought I'd owe one a debt. "Thank you for the protection, cow dog, perhaps I can pay you back."

She looked at me, closed her eyes, and sighed, "You look like cattle bait to me."

Bob White

CHAPTER SEVEN
The Other Brother

I wonder sometimes how places got their names. When Lewis and Clark headed west, they put tags on rivers and campsites all the way to the Pacific Ocean. But, the Indians and trappers must have had some names, too. How did the two explorers win the contest? They made the maps.

We all have stopped for people-type directions: "Go over two hills to the left turn, then a mile past that you'll see a red house. Go past the house to the second turn on your right, and watch for a big pine tree with a broken top. The place you're looking for is just beyond."

A map, on the other hand, puts names right there in front of you, showing the distance in miles, with numbers on roads and the streams in blue. Even if you can't find the place, it is still called something, on paper. The word has become history.

So, how do the map makers pick the names? Our northern county converted its whole geography with three numbers: 9-1-1.

Before that, the voice on one end of the telephone, in a high state of irritation and even panic, had to tell the dispatcher on the other end where, exactly, the fire trucks or deputy was to be sent. Unless the dispatcher knew where this particular Olson or that other Johnson lived, the caller ended up in the throes of "directions." The new system assigned each location a number and a street name. No matter that 2325 Fig Newton NW was seven miles up a dead-end road—everybody had an address that smacked of city sewer lines and street lights.

The job of naming the spiderweb strands in my neck of the woods fell to the Cass County Land Department. It was fortunate that this branch of county government has workers who are bright and creative. "Tree Frog Drive" is not the product of a dull mind. Nevertheless, every writer struggles for the right word. When the field workers were having an open moment, or if the name was contested by some homeowner, a few doors were knocked on for the residents' opinions:

"Ma'am, we are in the process of naming your road for the new 911 system. The name we have selected is Peabody Avenue. Will that be okay with you?"

"Absolutely not!" the woman states in seventy-year-old certainty. "Why would I want my road named after a guy that beats his wife?"

It is the end of a long day. The usual task of the tired survey worker is cruising timber under a green canopy of dancing, sun-lit leaves. No forestry professor prepared him for door-to-door opinion taking.

Then, in a moment of fatigue-born inspiration, the misplaced timber cruiser suggests, "How about Wife-Beater Road?"

"You got it, honey," and the door slams shut.

The origin of the name Mayo Creek has a higher tradition. The mapmaker was seeking to immortalize the names of Charles H. Mayo and his brother, William J. Mayo, famed surgeons and cornerstones of the world-renowned Mayo Clinic in Rochester, Minnesota. I don't know if the author of the map had ever been to the creek, but it, and its brother creek to the north, are worthy of their namesakes. They are pioneering flows of clear water, tracing their way south and east from the glacial moraine that formed the Maple Hills. They both turn and cut like a surgeon's blade between the rocks, watering the groves of poplar and oak woods until the main creek is slowed by a flat piece of soft ground, too spongy for cold-water slicing.

Here it is bent west because the knitted mass of a backwater valley has filled the pores of the earth, and the water's own weight pushes the stream back. The wet valley forms its own little drain, and the water refuses to join the main creek. It flows out of its spongy birthplace, growing a dense mat of alder in an aimless saunter; curls into a small amphitheater; and then, in its own good time, drips into North Mayo. This is the Other Brother, the ne'er-do-well stepchild Mayo, the mid-morning liaison of the milkman and the housemaid. How bad can it be? An illustration by story is required:

A pastor was compelled by conscience and tradition to conduct the funeral of a man known as a scoundrel, a blister, and an unrepentant layabout.

"Brothers and sisters!" he implored. "No man is without a virtue, all men are good and bad—some in small parts and some in large. Surely there is one among you in the congregation today who can find something good to say about the deceased!"

The plea was met with utter silence.

"One small thing, some kindness done, or smile made!"

Utter silence.

"Nothing at all, brothers and sisters, nothing to speed this sinner on his way?" the minister begged.

A throat cleared in the back of the church.

"Yes, citizen, yes. Tell it all!"

"Well," the voice said quietly, "his other brother wasn't half bad."

And so, the cover came to be named the Other Brother.

Now, the Other Brother never intended to be a Mayo Creek grouse cover. All it ever wanted to do was water the alder brush and swallow several hundred board feet of road corduroy every year. But the hard-rock farmer and the town board are relentless as well as persistent, and eventually a gravel road made its way across the spongy bog. A farmer scratched his fields out of the woods, and the timber cutters laid down the pine. The poplars filled the new openings, and with them came the grouse and the woodcock. The shiftless sponger had been forced to do some good.

If the poplar trees and the thick hazel clumps were magically lifted and swept out of the way to reveal the contour of the land, the eye would see an appearance like a wet-bottomed Dakota coulee. High land is present on each side, the shape flowing into a little basin like an amphitheater, with its open end toward the viewer. Empty of all the trees, sticks, tangles, and wait-a-minute vines, it would be about a forty-minute walk—and a rather dull one.

But put the shiftless and difficult nature of the cover back into place, and it is a full-day hunt, up one side and back down the other—most certainly not a stroll in the park. When Beans was younger and more inclined to cast wide and point beyond eyesight, I bought a blaze-orange vest that could be strapped around his body and clipped to his collar. It worked fine until we came in here. Halfway through the first hour he came back to see how I was doing. The vest was gone. That was three years ago. I know the blaze-orange cloth is in there, but I still haven't found it.

The cover is better now, but ten years ago one part could only be crossed by stepping from one downed tree to another. The grouse were in it and, as the old bank robber said, you go where the money is. But, you go prepared.

A lightweight shotgun is first. Regardless of gauge, it will be carried in one hand only. The other hand needs to push the brush aside and grasp for more. Jackets, in any form, are too hot to wear buttoned, are too loose when unbuttoned, and—when finally rolled up and stowed away—become a game-bag lump that gets caught in between saplings. This is a two-shirt cover: One to turn aside the first stab and the other for padding. If a grouse hunter peeled down to just a T-shirt under his vest, he would emerge looking as if he had been sorting cats. Gloves are indispensable. To paraphrase the credit-card ad: Don't leave home without them.

Experience taught me that I could expect birds anywhere but I could not expect to shoot them. For obvious reasons the best chances were on the town-road edge and then, after a few sightless flushes, in the interior, where the poplar sprouts had shaded away the competition.

Local lore still repeats a tale of a poacher spearing walleye and northern pike from the bank of Mayo Creek. The fish were running in thick schools, attracting the attention of other lawless elements. Being a single act, the one poacher was seized by three or four other poachers. A slender sapling about fifteen feet long was stripped of its branches and run through the hapless fellow's coat sleeves. His hands were tied to the wood shaft, and he was left in an area of dense regrowth, just like the Other Brother covert, to try and weave his way out.

Whether true, or apocryphal, this tale illustrates the difficulty of horizontal movement in a vertical world of young poplar trees.

Shotguns aren't fifteen feet long, but using them effectively to hit flying grouse requires horizontal movement. Grouse are short and can dodge along just fine, flying inside the poplar poles. They're safe as long as they don't fly straightaway or right back at the shooter. Swinging a shotgun after a bird in the Other Brother is like directing a band: up, down, over, up again, back down. Mostly, I just poke-shoot.

My hunting and shooting habits have been formed by the ruffed grouse and the stickery places it lives. Shooting instructors have never squinted over my shoulder. I am known, in polite shooting circles, as a bit ignorant.

That is not to say I am narrow minded or incapable of education. However, my technique is as subtle as "see 'em and knock 'em down"—more by faith, less by sight.

In the beginning I used a Model 31 Remington pump gun, the 1947 model with the big trigger guard and alloy frame. It tipped the scales at six pounds with a lightweight, straight-handed piece of Bishop walnut, plain as grass. I found a twenty-six-inch improved-cylinder barrel for it, locked that on the breech, and life was good. I needed nothing more, for I was then—and remain today—an unredeemed poke shooter.

It's not my fault. I was formed by my prey. The grouse that live here, ten miles from my home, have only one expectation: They expect to survive. To do this, they take off with a ripping whir, dodge between the trunks of nearby trees, and disappear behind the leafy screen.

I expect to kill them.

To do this I have to put a swarm of bird shot where they are going to be, just a heartbeat before they get there.

That is poke shooting.

I don't know how it is done. I don't think anyone could teach it. A clay pigeon might be able to a do a lot of dips and turns, but not between trees and not without smacking into one. My method is just picking a spot and filling it with a cloud of shot.

I don't see the barrels. I don't feel the gun at my shoulder. I just look at the spot and make it disappear in a burst of leaf debris and dust.

I used the Model 31 for a few years and then bought a Parker 12-gauge side-by-side with twenty-eight-inch barrels. It was a VH grade and had a stock with as much drop as a three-foot putt, but oh those barrels! They had a choke in each one that was pure poke-shooting poison. The patterns, when fired, appeared in heavy leaf debris as elliptical—oblong—left to right. I killed grouse that I had no business hitting, and in one memorable year, I took over one hundred.

But that gun was heavy, and in twenty years I got, somehow, older.

I took a few side roads, on one diversion acquiring a Browning Superlight superposed 20-gauge. I would have needed two shells to kill myself with it, but, it was just the currency for a trade with Griffin & Howe. I bought a Westley Richards 20-gauge side-by-side.

At five-and-a-half pounds, it is a little of everything but nothing too much. The gun was built in 1891, but, the twenty-six-inch barrels were made by Frederick Beesley sometime in the 1920s. The chokes are even, wide, and perfect at twenty yards on the right and maybe thirty yards on the left. And the wood! Glorious. With swirling bands of black, red, and gold, with a straight hand grip, it will poke shoot like lightning, In fact, the gun can kill with a glance.

On one occasion, Beans and I were moving through the

heavy alders of the Other Brother, pushing a cluster up to a grass center trail. On the other side of the trail was an open grazed pasture. I had just made it to the ditch when a grouse drove out of the dark-stemmed alders ahead of the dog and cleared the road.

It was flying in the hallway of the trail, and then it was dead in a puff of feathers, stone dead on the gravel.

"O-o-o-o-o h, Yes-s-s-s-s-s!"

We poke shooters are impulsive, direct, and not very subtle. We appreciate a shot like that when it all comes together.

The bird came back in Beans's mouth, and when I took it and smoothed its feathers, I quietly murmured, "I'll never make a finer shot." There was nothing left to be said.

On the other hand, there are the Other Brother's woodcock. Despite rumors of the demise of the species, may I say the rumors are a bit premature? I have never seen a flock of woodcock in migration, and I consider myself to be a pretty good and constant observer. They must fly alone. If they do, it would explain how, at certain times in the fall, the little bog sucker is so plentiful in this cover. The Other Brother must be the exact place at which each bird, winding its way along the Mayo Creek watershed, becomes so tired that it cannot rise above the sapling tops. Unable to maneuver farther, it strikes the whips and tumbles to the forest floor. There it lies, together with others of its kind, semicomatose, thickly littered like little wizened, brown apples in an orchard of one-stick trees.

I had to make a pact with my setter, Salty: If we got into the Other Brother's woodcock, I would shoot over every fifth point.

I didn't have to kill the bird, just shoot. Salty did not like to have her points ignored with shotless flushes. Unless I kept my part of the bargain, she would sulk and promptly bump the next grouse.

On the day I most remember, it was point, flush, walk four feet, point again. Two and sometimes three woodcock would flutter up the woody gray stripes, pause, flutter a little ways, and settle down again. I fired a few empty shots then—tiring of that—took the limit of five, separated by four points for each. I was being true to my word, but, a full three hours of grouse work lay before us. I did the only thing that made sense: I unloaded my gun, walked over, picked up Salty, and—with gun and bird dog tucked under my arm—threaded my way through the poplar poles until we came to the far edge.

I set her down, she shook it off, I reloaded, and we pressed on to a gray dogwood thicket in an old log landing. The roots that send up the dense growth of poplar suckers must have been damaged, or the gray dogwood just beat out the competition. The sun-loving bushes filled the opening, spreading themselves among the surviving hardwoods. If grouse hunting ever had a guarantee, this spot came with that and a warranty. Birds guaranteed, and warranted never to be seen.

Big dogwood thickets top out at about eight feet. Grouse flushing out of big dogwood thickets top out at eight feet, six inches. My hunting partner on that day was Bill Habein, a kindred soul with an even pace and fine manners.

"Bill!" I called out, "I can see a bird in front of Salty."

The grouse was standing upright, a gray brown triangle motionless under the canopy. It bobbed its head, turned, and started to walk off. Salty stepped forward in a small catlike movement. The bird froze tight.

"I'm going to push it out. Be ready."

"Okay," he answered, "but it's thick."

Holding the little 20-gauge by its straight grip, I reached out and lifted the biggest branch, made one long stride, and dropped the limb behind me. The bird lifted up, straight through the overhang and out of sight.

"Bird's up!" I shouted. There was no shot.

"Ted, you'd better come and look at this," came a muffled voice on the other side of the clump.

Bill was standing, his gun at the ready, looking up into a large old poplar tree. The late afternoon sky was white, overcast and brooding about a forecasted storm. There, silhouetted on several limbs were five ruffed grouse, a whole tree full.

I don't know how it is in other areas, but in this country if a local knows you hunt grouse he will inevitably tell you about the famous grouse tree. The numbers of birds in that tree can vary with the fudge factor of the teller, but always the result is the same: The shooter starts at the bottom and works his way to the top, killing them all and taking care that none falls in front of the others (this will startle them, you see). He uses anything from a 12-gauge shotgun to a deer rifle to the generic ".22." It is the story that is guaranteed to follow any inquiry of: "Didja get any?"

"There's five grouse up there," he said in wonderment. "Can you believe it?"

"And one more over here on the ground under Salty's point," I added.

"What now?" Bill asked.

He and I have a rule: We don't shoot grouse out of trees. It is more fun to have one of us at the ready and the other throwing sticks or, better yet, shaking the tree. This one was too big to shake. A grouse diving out of a tree is a hard shot for the outside guy. If the tree is shakable, however, the volunteer under the dropping bird has almost a straightaway.

"Tell you what. I'll walk over and flush up this pointed bird. When I shoot they should all bail out."

"Good luck," Bill replied.

"Same to you."

I had chosen the easiest opportunity. I could tell from the way Salty held her head that she was looking at the grounded bird. Fortunately I couldn't see it. If I see them on the ground, I usually miss.

When the grouse flushed I knew it was dead. It was a young bird, a short-tailed brown phase with a ragged comb. Those kind of details can only be seen when the target is in center focus.

I didn't hear my shot, but I heard Bill shoot twice. Four dark arrows flew between the leaf openings, heading for deeper places.

"Get one?" I asked.

"Yes, on the second shot. The first one was a waste," he answered.

"They can be close in here," I said.

Close is a relative term. In the Other Brother, nothing is ever far away. It can't be. A man can't see farther than six feet. The end of the cover is the Amphitheater. The water, shiftless as its namesake, lacked the energy to push dirt out of the way. So in the basin it curled around and waited to spill out through the adjoining pasture from the natural bowl shape. Bird movement seems to be naturally concentrated toward the center. The trees in here are larger, and game animals have made their paths to and from the seep in the bottom.

I was walking down a deer path looking under brush tops for a wisp of white tail or a patch of Salty's flank. Her bell had stopped, and I did not have a good mark on the location.

"Bird's up!" Bill shouted from the perimeter.

I stopped and turned toward the sound. Up, and coming in a swooping turn, a single grouse was on top of me before I could raise the gun. It flared its wings, dropped the landing flaps, and settled to the ground less than a foot away.

It looked up. "*Puck, puck, puck,*" it said, in that irritated sound a grouse utters when it has made a huge mistake.

"I guess to hell," I replied.

"Flush! Go on, get outta here!" I yelled. And it did—on foot.

I suppose that grouse figured that it had botched up the job of flying so badly that running was the only option left. Try as I might, I could not get through the heavy stems fast enough to either chase it up or kick it up. The bird simply walked away.

"Did you see that one go by?" Bill asked as he came around a clump of brush and sat down on a nearby log.

"See it? Yes, and if it had been any closer I could have married it! But it ran away."

"Heh, heh, heh," he chuckled, "probably a female."

The Other Brother. If a wildlife biologist wanted an illustration of what a cover would look like if everything was planned wrong and designed badly, he couldn't find a better example. But like directions given by mouth, the number of birds in it proves that there is more than one way to get the job done.

CHAPTER EIGHT
Bob and Rosie

I love the color of bug lights.

No, not the blue zappers with the wire lattice. I'm talking about yellow lightbulbs, like the ones that lined the eaves of the A&W root-beer stand on hot summer nights. It was behind the old hotel, a four-floor, square brick building that used to sit on a lot that now displays new Chevrolets.

Everyone in town gathered there in the summer, in a yellow haze of moths and reflected light—rows upon rows of cars. Ten cents bought a frosted mug holding more root beer than a kid could drink. Every time I look at the car lot I can see the chopped and channeled 1950s hot rods. Especially one driven by the most radical human I had ever seen. A young man with a Mohawk haircut, a real small-town character. But the guy with the Mohawk had nothing on Bob.

I have lunch almost every day in the same cafe. By the time I sit down on the second stool from the end of the counter, a sandwich—made from the day's special, on wheat bread, and served with two peanut-butter cookies—is up in the cook's window, with a cup of strong black coffee.

"You must call ahead, counselor," said Bob one day as he sat on the next stool.

I am always happy to have lunch next to Bob. Slender and springy as a whip, he has bright eyes that twinkle under gray eyebrows. Or, they can flash like fire when his Irish temper flares. Bob is purely unpredictable. I know for a fact that he once pulled a disc plow with his Oldsmobile. "I sold the pickup," was his answer, and that was that.

"No, Bob, I'm just a creature of habit," I answered.

We got to talking about cars and then old cars and, finally, old times. The yellow lights of summer and the root-beer stand came around about the time I was dunking my peanut-butter cookies in the coffee.

"That used to be where the icehouse for the hotel stood," he explained. "I spent most of a night in there."

"In an icehouse? It must have been a hot night," I said.

The waitress passed along the counter and poured coffee for us.

"A couple of buddies and I had spent the early and middle part of an evening in the beer joint up the road. One thing led to another, and what with being thirsty from haying all afternoon I overfilled a bit. Well, they couldn't take me home in that condition, and since I fell asleep, they carried me to the car. One of them worked at the hotel on the night shift. So, when we all drove into the back, the guy apparently said, "Let's haul Bob into the icehouse and lay him down. That ought to sober him up, and I'll come out later to check."

Knowing Bob, I started to chuckle and said, "I'll bet he forgot."

"He did. Sometime in the early morning I started to come around. At first, I couldn't figure out where I was or what season I was in. I was freezing cold. I tried to move, but my arms and legs were so stiff from lying on the sawdust-covered ice blocks that I couldn't."

"I must be dead!" I thought.

Bob's blue eyes twinkled as I laughed out loud, dropping my cookie on the counter.

"Then I said, 'I'm not dead and I got to move, or I *will* die!' So I rocked a little to the right and then a little to the left, and finally I toppled off the ice blocks onto the dirt floor. I heard a car go by and figured out where I was."

"Were you sobered up?" I asked.

"Stone cold sober," he answered, and we both guffawed.

Bob's people owned a farm that was split by Mayo Creek. Pushed west by the soggy weight of the Other Brother, the rush of water passed under the old roadway through two culverts. It found some soft ground on its journey and kept the westerly heading until the hard shoulder of a rocky ridge turned the flow south again. From there to Bob's far grass pasture, the water washed from stone to stone, spilling out in the many small pools and accumulating a rich, black bottomland. River birches sprouted as did low, lush shade-lovers like ferns and the little green plants that grouse like to eat.

Bob cut the trees along the westerly course of the Mayo and, like his neighbors, piled the stumps and brush in rows to make cattle fairways between the piles. He leveled his side of the southbound creek, leaving the opposite side to grow thick and wild. As the years passed, the crop fields stayed on the level ground above the stream, and Bob fenced the cattle into the rocky bottom. Gray dogwood, hazel brush, and other good bird bushes filled the spaces between the cow paths. Like all rough-ground farmers before him, he created better habitat by accident than most wildlife managers could on purpose.

The settlers needed a place to put their dead. A cemetery was created across the road from the Other Brother, inside Bob's farm. At about four square acres, it has one side along the windrows, one side to the road. The other side, and the back, are bordered by fields that are usually planted in corn. The trees in the grave-yard are very old—some pine, a few oak, spared the saw by the settlers who reserved a piece of the country they were trying to tame. The headstones are also old, overgrown with weeds, fox-tail, and hay grass. There are no statues or urns in this quiet place. And, somewhere in here, maybe under the wind-broken oak limb, large enough to be a tree in itself, are the graves of a mother and three children, all buried on the same day.

The *Amanita phalloides* is the destroying angel of the mush-room family. Gathering berries and mushrooms was a common enough practice in Norway. Perhaps the *Amanita* looked like an old-country edible. What was intended to be some extra food for the supper pot, gathered by a mother and her children, took their lives by sunrise. The mother, it is said, being physically larger, survived the longest. But dizzy, faint, and blind, she could only tell her returned husband that something was wrong with the children and that he should find help. But the poison had by then put her beyond reach, and she slowly succumbed, as the children already had.

The same death-cup mushroom can be found next to the cemetery fence in the first windrow of Bob's Mayo Creek cover. As I crushed it under my boot sole, I recalled the ironic twist of fate. The *Amanita,* lethal to humans, was just another piece of forage to the grouse I held in my hand. The first bird of my day had been picking its breakfast along the woven wire fence separating the rough and brushy rows from the graves. When Salty came upon the grouse, she simply stopped, raised her tail, and turned her head to the left.

The fence was on the top edge of the Mayo Creek Valley. Refuge was downhill, and that was where the bird wanted to go. As it climbed above the small trees I just followed up its tail with my lead hand, pulled ahead of the beak, and pressed the stock to my face. The grouse collapsed into a loose bundle, wings flopping, and fell into the adjoining trees. Within a moment, Salty's black Labrador servant had retrieved the bird to me for examination.

Bill Habein was with me again, downhill, waiting quietly for the results. There had been one shot, and he was close enough to hear me tell Jet to bring back the bird.

As a longtime hunting partner, he knew without asking that

I was opening the crop to see what the grouse were eating.

"Clover and mushrooms," I called out.

"Okay," came the response, "I've got some down here, too."

I spilled the white chunks of toadstool on the ground and ground them into the dirt with my foot. "Well, pilgrims, I guess this proves, again, that mushrooms are dangerous business on every side of the food chain."

"What did you say?" Bill called.

"Nothing, I was just talking to the graveyard," I answered.

Bill had a springer spaniel for several years. Her first name was "Rosie." Her middle initial was "U," and her last name was hyphenated in true, liberated, modern style as "Sonoffa-Bitch." At least that is what it sounded like; I never saw it written out.

Rosie did not run through heavy brush. The term "boiled" comes to mind. She boiled through the woods. It's hard to describe the effect of that sturdy body on standing vegetation, but things flew into the air—sticks, leaves, grass, loose branches, and even grouse. Hunting with Rosie was not a subtle application of anything. Her accelerator was buried to the floor, and she was 100 percent committed to seeking, flushing, retrieving, and unleashed spaniel enthusiasm.

Common sense tells us that pointing dogs and flushing spaniels don't go together in the field. It's like mixing assault troops and spies. That did happen, on occasion, but far less than often. So Bill and I divided the grouse covers into different areas. If the going was thick and the leaf screen heavy, my small, white setter was hard to find. This was spaniel country. Jet would join

Rosie, and the two dogs would flush the creek-bottom grouse, forcing them up and out of the sticks. If Salty had one on point in that thick soup, it got busted. I don't think she minded.

Salty was aware of the difficulty I had in finding her. If her bell had been quiet for that certain space of time equaling a point, I could call to her, softly, saying: "Salty, shake!" Shortly afterward, I would hear the bell quietly tinkle. If the interval went too long, she had patented a technique of her own. She learned how to tree the bird.

I never saw exactly how she did this, but once accomplished, she would circle the tree and bark until I came. After this happened a few times, one of my Missouri hunting companions sent me a magazine when he got home. The title of it was "Full Cry," and the cover showed a hound dog with a coon in a tree.

The mushroom bird was safely stored in my vest bag and I continued to walk the ridge top. The sound of Bill's shot bounced back from the creek-side trees. I paused and listened for his voice.

"Woodcock," he called. Rosie was stirring up the alder bottom.

The graveyard fence came to the end of the cornfield, where the cover thins. At this point I walked down two rows to get back into the heavier brush. I couldn't hear my dog. The bell was quiet.

"Salty, shake!" I called softly.

"*Ka-POW!*" I jumped in surprise.

"Grouse!" came the yell from below. On cue and from stage right, a bird cleared the six feet of air over the windrow and was framed in the open alleyway. I swept it out of the sky and sent Jet off to pick it up. Then I could see that Salty was on point, just in front of me on the other side of a clump of hazel brush. One shell in the left tube, a tighter choke. Should I break the gun and reload the open barrel?

No, this grouse had my number and was waiting for a mistake. I stepped out from behind the bush. It was very close, but instead of coming directly into my face the grouse followed its outstretched head up into the sky. I knew where it was going and put my last shot into that spot. Three birds down in as many shots. It was going to be a very fine morning.

"Woodcock!" came from down low, followed by a second shot. Bill was having a good bird boil.

We were coming to the end of the rows. There were two old apple trees, sour crabby ones, pushing out of a rock pile by a wire gate on the ridge fence. Salty was getting a drink from the creek, and Bill had a few more yards to come. I swung the little Westley Richards 20-gauge up and back and forth, practicing a bit. At just over five pounds, the little gun was wonderful to carry, but it was weak on crossing shots. Light guns are easy to stop swinging.

"Just like that," I thought, and swung it through again, right to left, "just like that." At that instant a grouse flushed from the creek, and up the bank, skimming the fence top. The bird was a wide open, fast crosser at extreme open-choke range, heading back toward the graveyard, bright and clear against the cornfield sky.

I swept the little gun through its line, never measuring the lead, just getting out front, bringing the stock to my face, and pressing the trigger. The bird dropped its head against its chest and somersaulted in the air, once, twice, and crashed.

If the rush of elation I felt could be manufactured, it would have to be licensed. "Grouse!" I yelled. "Just like that!" Give me a couple warm-ups and I can do anything.

Rosie came up out of the jungle, flying ears and joy, followed in a minute or two by Bill. "Get him?" he asked and sat down on a stump.

"Oh yeah," I answered, "I made my once in a season shot, how about you?"

"A grouse and three woodcock," he said. "You have two then?"

I shook my head, and lifted four gloved fingers in the air.

"Oh man," he nodded his head in a broad, bearded grin, "four shots, four birds; the little gods are in your pocket today."

And, in his, too. We finished our pipes and were checking pockets and shell loops when Rosie came back from the other side of her trip around the world. (Rosie did not take breaks.) She flushed a woodcock off the very end of the last row. It twittered up, a long shot, and then banked away to increase the distance. Sometimes a bird sends a message, otherwise two hunters wouldn't shoot the same bird out of a flock. This one must have spoken to Bill; he lifted his 20-gauge over-and-under in one smooth, mount and shoot motion. The little brown dot dropped, stoned, struck by lightning.

"Don't move, I want to measure this off!" I said.

Forty-five paces to where the small feathers lay scattered in the grass. It was a miracle shot, almost an act of God. We would need it as a balance for what was to come.

As Rosie became older, she did not slow down as we thought she might. Instead she would suddenly wind down, stagger, and flop—trembling—onto the ground. Bill figured that it was a blood-sugar condition and concocted some glucose-rich snacks. The year before this one, the food worked. With her jet fuel on board, she was back to full bore. But, on the second day after the opener, she hit the wall.

The weather was hot. The first day had proved that, and we had laid up for most of that afternoon, glad to be out of the heavy leaf screen. We made plans to hunt Bob's land along Mayo Creek, starting early before the humidity and heat came on the day.

Salty—and even Jet, to a lesser degree—was skilled in pacing herself. She had an even, rocking-chair gait, never tearing here and there, just exploring in her smooth, seamless fashion each bushy corner and likely hiding place.

Rosie had lost that page of the bird-dog hunting book. She probably tore it out and ate it. But mother nature has a hard bosom and little tolerance for feckless fools, especially aging ones.

The humidity was pumped up by a heavy dew. When the sun finally touched the forest floor, it steamed, coloring the air a light blue. There was no scent drifting in smoky trails for a pointing dog. The bird work was down and dirty, our shirts plastered to our backs, and our buckskin gloves soaked black on our hands.

It was just noon. Bill and I may have shot a bird or two, but I don't remember that. I recall standing on the creek bank pushing the dogs back into the swishing water to cool them down.

"Let's knock off," I said. "If we cross the creek right here we can walk straight up the other bank, through the brush clumps, and out onto the pasture. Then it's only a couple of hundred yards to the trucks."

"Right. It must be eighty degrees today," Bill said.

We started out side by side, but after the climb up onto the brushy flats, Bill lagged back.

"Rosie is stumbling along," he said. "She is spent."

By the time I was out in the pasture, Bill had slowed to walk beside the liver-and-white spaniel. Her tongue was lolling, and her head was hanging low. She dropped her feet in front of her like bricks, first to one side, then to the other.

"I'll go ahead and unlock my truck," I called back.

Bill waved his hand, gesturing me on.

I was busy with the small details of unlocking the tailgate and putting my gun away, and I did not hear him yell the first time. But I heard it the second time.

"Ted! Ted! Come quick, she's dead!"

Bill was on his knees. Even at two hundred yards I could see one arm extended to cradle a limp white bundle and the other gesturing frantically. Have you seen that famous photograph of the Kent State co-ed bending over the dead classmate? That's what I saw: slack-mouthed, stunned disbelief.

My soft drink can arched away, thrown aside to the right, as I ran toward my two friends. I was never much of a runner, and closing the distance seemed to take so long. Bill was pulling me on with his arm, the blood roaring in my ears and my throat full of fear.

I tried to remember what to do. Check the eyes? Fixed and dilated. Then, check the mouth, clear the airway. Her gums were gray, and her chest was not moving. Bill's eyes were stunned with horror.

"On her back, put her on her back!" But what did I know about resuscitating dogs? I had done this on wounded men on the hard, red ground of Con Thien. This was a dog!

Sounds odd, but there isn't a lot of difference, at least in how it feels. Most soldiers had moustaches. When you clamp your mouth down to breathe life out of death, hard little whiskers stab your lips. You'd think in the heat of action little things like that wouldn't register. But they do, in fact, they're about all that really stays after the chopper flies away.

It felt pretty much the same, but my breath blew out the sides of Rosie's muzzle. Bad seal—got to lock it up! I pulled her lips together and held her jaws in both my hands, then pulled her throat straight, turning her head to one side. I took a deep breath and blew hard. Her chest rose. I blew again, and it rose three times, then four, and five. Nothing.

I put my hand on the V-shape where the ribs meet. "Push here," I said to Bill. "Count them, ten times."

He counted out loud. I held up my hand, "Wait, I'll try again."

One more breath and another, her eye just inches from mine, and . . . the pupil moved!

"We got it!" Her eye squeezed down to pin size, then opened slightly. She moved her head and started to pant.

"Get the water!" It was Bill's turn to run.

Then he was back. I know he ran the two hundred yards to the truck, dug for his keys, opened the back, got the jug, and ran back. I just don't recall his being gone.

He poured it through her mouth and all over her body. Slowly, slowly, she rolled onto her belly, then pushed herself to a sitting position and panted some more.

"Let's take her into the shade between the trucks and see if she can walk," I said.

She could, and the springer followed Bill and me, a little unsteady, all the way.

I spread out my blanket, then got my lunch, found the drink can still half full, and sat down with my back against the tire. My dogs had crawled in back. Rosie lay quietly with her chin between her paws. Bill sat across from me, his back resting against his own truck.

A long space passed. Probably the universe making an adjustment for all that activity packed into one small part.

"Ted, thanks, I just wanted to say . . . "

"No, don't bother, it all came to some good." I replied.

More time, small movements, then I said, "Where do we go from here?"

"Nowhere," Bill replied, "I lost my truck keys."

CHAPTER NINE
The Promised Land

God, I can push the grass apart
And, lay my finger
On thy heart.

—Edna St. Vincent Millay

"A truly fine grouse cover," he began, "has, like a beautiful woman, a distinct and recognizable shape. But that, in itself, is not enough. In addition to its obvious beauty, it must have a covering—a skin, if you will—that is unique. It is this that attracts the hunter's attention. If it is not present then it is just another body. Finally, there must be a quality of moisture that is more like a rivulet—a small track of passion—to flow in that valley. There is no place here for the standing pool or flowing river.

"The hills serve the necessary function of elevation. A grouse requires a wide variety of foods—some upland and some lowland—and the bird will seek both kinds at different times of the day. The gray dogwood grows best on a sunny, upland hillside, but that small three-leaved green plant that the birds were eating today can only be found where the ground is low and cool. Which brings me to the bird's habit of seeking the highlands when it is freezing in order to stay out of the heavy cold air, and then the cool areas to escape the heat. A truly fine covert has round outlines and sensuous curves.

"I have struggled through stretches of ground that can only be called heartless bitches. These have long grass in old alders. Every step must be knee high or better in order to get over the fallen wood. Shin bones are stabbed by broken stumps, and the ground is lumped up and often soggy. A good dog is compelled to crawl and twist through the mess to find the few birds that live there.

"Some hills are flat and stingy. I have found these so covered with downed trees that the only way across was to step from trunk to trunk. Even worse, I have tripped in these places and been unable to fall because the brush held me up.

"No, the skin of a truly fine bird covert has clover in its openings and berry bushes along its edges. The trees are never just one age. There are some older aspens to provide winter food and younger ones close by to give the birds protection from hawks and owls. There should also be an occasional spruce tree to provide an umbrella against the rain and snow, and to give a warm ceiling on a cold night before the snow gets deep enough. It is a nurturing element for a smooth easy life.

"There has to be moisture, too. Nothing soggy, you understand. A small brook moving over some rocks, with a source from a beaver pond, perhaps, or a spring. The valley provides shelter from the harsh wind, and it gives the hunter a point to start from and return to. Such a place organizes the cover into manageable parts. The birds can settle upon territories and divide themselves into coveys. The hunter can name one side or the other and walk this one in a particular way and the other in a different manner. The dogs have a source of water, and on a hot day someplace to lie down and cool off."

*   *   *

A grouse covert described as a beautiful woman . . . the voices in this narrative were fictitious when I wrote it several years ago, but the place they describe is real.

A small tributary feeds into Mayo Creek from the south. It starts as a seep from some underground source and runs north. Above ground, it appears as a pasture pool in one spot and a wet swamp in another, until the land falls away in a slope that is steep enough to wash a gully. This small stream winds its way, unnamed, through the woods until it meets the wet nose of a beaver. Cast out of his home pond in the spring, he has settled here, in a place where he can build a dam across a narrow opening.

The cleavage in the full bosom I described is that place, a narrow wooded valley between two round hills. If the old town road was the waistline, then the pond would be the flat, smooth belly of my maiden, rising and falling with the spring rain, trickling the clear surface of her sheen over the edge of the dam and across the stones of the valley bottom. A sparkling tumble spreads where the crest of each hill tapers, stirring the earth into a shallow depression where the neck meets the hard-earth collarbone of the Mayo. The lesser gods that dwell here must be female because walking its soft, round, and pleasing contours affects me in a visual and physical way.

On the east side there is a gate. It is a battered and bent frame of twisted iron hanging from its swing post by one hinge. At first I thought it was just part of the old wood corral. One noon, curious to see why there was a slot in the woods behind the fence, I pushed it open. There was a trail. Not an obvious road, just the faintest change in texture, with blackberry bushes on each side and tall grass between. I walked ten or twelve yards and stopped. The slot was now an alley, framed on each side by aspen trees. I walked some more, stopping to pick the ripe berries, and where the trees shaded the sunlight the path widened. It became a field road, the sort of driveway that remains in places where the grass cannot cover the hard dirt tire lines.

There is a small aster that flowers in the sand of old fields. It was September and its bushy carpet was a fog of pale blue cloud banks marking the last efforts of a lost homestead. One of these fields had been scratched out of an opening beyond the poplar grove. A run of alder bordered the far edge drawing me across until I could see a hole in the leafy wall, another segment of the road in a green tunnel, and beyond that more sunlight.

I knew that the pond stretched from the road to the sparkling edge of the beaver dam. It was in front of me, but the clear land on the other side of the tunnel had the same blue tops as the field I was standing in.

Salty and Jet had been sleeping under the truck when I pushed the gate open. We had spent our morning across the road, hunting the cow trails and pasture edges of the neighboring land. One, or the other, had shaken awake and now both came thundering past, glad to be part of a new adventure. They ran through the tunnel and instead of disappearing with a splash into water, chased each other up a slight rise, pausing to look back.

"A second field," I thought. "In all the time I hunted through the low ground on the other side, I thought I was looking out on a reed-grass swamp."

Salty came back toward me a few steps, but Jet charged on up the hill and over to the other side. The tunnel was dark and cool; on both sides of the old road, boards had been placed on edge, with wooden stakes behind and earth packed between. Here and there out in the heavy growth, water sparkled in small puddles, but the land rose into a clear mound. I made the top and stood, cap in hand, scratching my head, studying the basement hole of a long gone home. Built on about four acres of sand and gravel, the little homesite was surrounded by the pond and bordered on three sides by tall golden reeds. Laid out before me, across the whole horizon, was the resplendent beauty of my maiden. Ducks swam and dabbled for the wild-rice kernels, and a cool breeze pressed the aster bushes in a bow and curtsy from one to the other.

Bird dogs speak with the lesser gods, and even though I had that tight, happy feeling under my belt buckle, I had to ask the setter if I was right.

"Salty, if there is a heart in the earth, then surely this must be its place," I said.

She didn't answer, of course, but she didn't have to. She was rolling and rubbing her body against the ground, her eyes closed in the pure pleasure of it.

The road was solid enough to drive. The next day my pickup pushed the alder branches out of the green tunnel and circled the house hole. I unloaded an old pirogue duck boat and a bag of decoys, stowing them in the tall grass between the pond water and the dry ground. There were still some mallard ducks puddling along the far shore, and a good-sized flock had jumped when I drove up. The next morning was a Monday, but I had from sunrise to at least 8 A.M. before my work would draw me back to town. I didn't even have to make a blind. The tall reeds and heavy swamp grass along the edge would swallow up my form.

On the following day, it was just Jet and me in the dark. The sun would rise early on the cornfield behind me, and with no cloud cover to deaden the light, things would be over about a half an hour after the rays brightened the yellow poplar across the water. I had paddled the little skiff out from the shore about thirty yards and had set only a dozen mallard decoys and six wood-duck blocks. No birds had risen when I drove in, and none surprised me as I set the blocks. A bad sign.

We waited through one cup of coffee, a pipe, and another

cup. Four wood ducks swept the pond from road to dam, but crested the trees and kept going.

"A classic duck hunter's morning, Jet," I said, "fall colors, quiet water, a clear sky, and no ducks." I poured my third cup of coffee. If I had brought a sandwich it would have been time for that, too. "The only thing left to bring them in is to pick up the decoys."

I set the Thermos back on the ground and was searching for a dropped glove when I heard Jet whine lightly. My eyes followed her set gaze. Two white gliders were banking around the wild rice bed, setting their wings to land.

"Lord have mercy!" I whispered; they looked like airliners. I had seen swans in the late fall, flying over my deer stand, and had sometimes spotted them on the big lakes, but never in a little pothole like this one. And never so close.

They landed and swam into the decoys, side by side. One had an orange band on its wing, close to the body. These had to be trumpeter swans. There are lots of long-necked white birds on the earth, like snow geese and tundra swans, but nothing could look like this. There was room for twin engines.

One talked quietly, playing notes on a deep woodwind instrument. Its black bill merging with its eye, the other turned its head as if to study the little duck shapes. Something was not quite right. They discussed it and, coming to a decision, swam out of the spread. There they paused, idling a moment. Then, still together, they lifted off, trotting down the waterway, their great long wings rippling the morning like bedsheets shaken from the clothesline. Jet jumped to her feet and ran to the water's edge. I stood up, trying to keep them in sight for just a little longer.

"Wow, and all I had in mind was a few shots at ducks." The morning was made but not over. As the sun cleared the trees behind the low round-topped mound, it carried its yellow light to the poplar and maple leaves on the far side. Like the unveiling of a master work of art, the shroud of early morning fell down to the water, and in its place was the image of every fall landscape ever painted, only alive, not fixed in oil pigments.

I am here and I am allowed to see this? A small idea born of a noontime walk and a truck full of scratched-up hunting gear hauled out in the flat light of full day were the humble origins that had given birth to a singular life moment. It was more than just color and light; it was communication. It was a message between gods. It was, however, one intended for me to see—and recall, as well.

Within a week my Missouri friends arrived for the grouse and woodcock. We put in two days of hard hunting, and in the evening of the second we decided, upon my suggestion, to spend a morning at the pond, set out some decoys, and watch the sun come up. They had never been to the old homesite, and the weather promised a clear sky.

"I think we'll see something worth going out for," I said, and everyone put in early. They stayed in a little log cabin that I have for guests. As I walked back to the house my vertically impaired and rotund biologist friend, Spencer Turner, said his dad was seriously ill and unlikely to last the year. I could sympathize. The phone had rung at 4 A.M. on Christmas morning for me, only a couple years ago. My dad had passed away, the nurse said. I sat on the bed. There were calls to make and busy things to do, but at 4 A.M., death is not diluted by the tasks of the day. It sits next to you.

I had set my alarm for 6 A.M. on the morning of our duck hunt. The trucks were packed; breakfast would be after the morning was wrapped up. The bell rang, but it was not my alarm; it was the phone. It was Spencer's sister. His dad had died; please inform Spencer; etc. etc. Yes, of course, I'll see to it. (I'm almost an expert.) The time was 4 A.M.

I could see the cabin windows from my bedroom. It was dark, two hours from wake-up time. Spence's dad lived in Wisconsin, miles away. He would have to leave, make calls, do busy things. It could wait. He would not forget a detail of the moment of death's message. I wanted him to remember it differently.

I am not a morning person; neither is Spence, so the ride out to the battered iron gate was quiet. He pushed it open for our vehicle and one other, climbed back into the truck, and in two vehicles, one behind the other, we pressed through the blackberries and alder tunnel to circle the house hole and park. The gear was tossed out onto the ground, the boat turned over, the decoys arranged. It all took time. Time enough for the sun to color the sky behind us, time enough for coffee, time to talk of small things, and time to sit quietly on canvas stools waiting for the light.

It was, as before, a perfect duck morning, the quiet steam of our breathing just floating in the air before us. Then, as before, the very tip of each tree was lighted. The shroud dropped, yellow and red became the fire of fall, and the water gave back the reflection.

"Wow!" I heard Spence say. "Look at that!"

My eyes brimmed up and my nose started to burn. At first my voice caught in a short hitch, and I think that is what caught his attention.

"Spence," I said, "I have some hard news for you, but I wanted you to hear it here because you are never going to forget the words or the place you heard them." My throat tightened up, but I willed myself to say it:

"Your dad died this morning."

His head dropped, then he lifted his eyes to the trees. I turned my gaze away and stared at the ground. A single tear dropped through the air, marking my rubber boot with its spatter. Spence stood, placed his hand on my shoulder, nodded, and said, "Thank you, that was exactly right."

He walked back up into the field. In a short while, one of the other fellows came over from his blind.

"Did I hear right?" he asked. I was surprised that my voice had carried, but maybe it hadn't. A message like that is as old as mankind and travels great distances.

"Yeah, Spence's dad died this morning. I got the call at 4 A.M."

He looked around, his face lit in the sun's straight light. It was a tapestry of color, and peace. "That's exactly how I would have wanted to hear it." He walked out of the grass and up the hill to his friend.

Communicated by voices we shall never hear, some messages are not intended for human ears. Some are, but in voices we once heard but lost. The lesser gods that dwell in places like this paint pictures worth thousands of unspoken words.

*   *   *

My connection with this place, my Promised Land, is deep and personal. The records at the County Recorder state quite concisely that it is a tract of 240 acres, consisting of six 40-acre parcels, two deep and three long. The data gathered by the United States Agricultural Service show 70 acres of hay pasture, a pond, a creek drainage, and "the balance in hardwood forest."

They are not wrong. I just look at things here differently. I think about certain grouse covers in their objective way. They are productive because the habitat is right. I hunt them, and I harvest the birds. If I have guests, we go to these covers. It is not so personal. Those birds don't speak to me, the small voices on the breeze don't say "turn here," or "sit on this log, and look over there."

Deep within me, when I am in this land, is the knowledge that something knows I am here. Something knows and cannot be fled from or hid from—not a sinister thing but a harmony. You are one of us, it says, and I will look out for you and those you love.

Oliver Gravley, my old friend, the man who led me here, was killed on the side of a small hill in the Promised Land. Oliver loved to cut firewood, but he forgot that under nature's law, whimsical fate and accident rule the universe. He cut a tree, and it fell into another. He undercut that one, and it, too, hung up. Oliver must have been tired, and this frustrated him. Then, as the music from the radio in the cab of his pickup truck played through the open door, he cut the third tree, and the first one slid down the slanted trunk of its neighbor and killed him.

The radio music played, the breeze rustled the leaves, an announcer talked about the weather until the battery went dead and the woods were quiet again. A year later I passed through the spot. The scattered chunks of cut wood still lay where Oliver left them; so did the three trees, one over the other. There was one other thing I had never seen before that sunny afternoon. Cattle from the pasture had come up into the woods. They were lying down in that place, quiet and peaceful. Oliver loved cattle, probably in the same way that I love the grouse that live here. I keep that image of him.

His son, Ken, is a friend and a man whom I like and respect. Ken is not a bird hunter nor a deer hunter. The land became his and in keeping with a promise made to me years ago, he sold it to me. It is a dangerous thing to love a place so much. Better, really, to relate to the land as a surface that provides the thing we seek. Then if it is lost to another, there can always be another place. After all, money is just a medium of exchange. Or is it?

Alas, for the lifelong battle
Whose bravest slogan is bread.

These are not my words; they are better than any I could think of, though, to express that there are places on this earth worth more than the sum of what it takes to buy them.

Is the Promised Land a gift of the gods? It must be. How else could so many small things harmonize, to welcome me here and reward me every bird season. Can men be lesser gods? Some can, especially those who hold the land and pass it on to those that love it.

Bob White

CHAPTER TEN
The Tie that Binds

On a still evening, sitting on the tailgate with a cup of coffee and the contented snoring of my bird dog, I can feel a harmony, a soft squeeze in the middle of my body. It's a quiet, tight place under my heart, telling me to listen as the migrating robins cluck from gray dogwood thickets, counting the minutes it takes the sun to set.

I wish I could say that there is also a flash of light, a burning bush, or some other miraculous conversion. There isn't. I am the same old girl I used to be. As the song says—the same old walk, the same old talk, the same old off the wall. And, I still fall back into bad habits. In the company of competitive hunters, I compete. In the face of bad shooting or busted points, I despair. But I have more quiet moments than I used to, and with each passing season I am bound more tightly to this land by the experiences I have here.

I own a bird dog named Beans. A lot of lip service is paid out on the theme "I'm in it for the dog work; I really don't care if I get anything." I'll believe that when the speaker leaves his gun behind. Good dog work is a gift, and a hunter never really knows how his new prospect is going to turn out. Beans had big shoes to fill, which is amazing considering how small Salty was. Like any fine dog, she laid down a high standard of performance. I knew what fine dog work was because Salty taught me. Beans would have been better off as my first dog.

He had one thing in his favor: he was a completely different breed. Salty was an English setter. Beans is a German shorthair. He has predatory lines—sleek, muscular, with a fine, square head. He looks nothing like the wiry, bony, bundle of pure grouse sense that was Salty.

Salty trained two Labrador retrievers to hunt grouse with her. It was my hope that she had one more year left in her to train Beans. It was not to be. Beans was on his own.

There is a road I call the Center Trail in the middle of the Promised Land. It divides the cover in two parts by traveling from the gate to the fence bordering Mayo Creek. The best grouse cover is right at the beginning. On our first hunt there, Beans blew through two birds without a blink. He was interested—that part was good—and he proved it by chasing them almost all the way to the pond. That was not so good. We had worked hard on pigeons, road-killed grouse, and pen-raised quail. He had the instinct to point and was solid and stylish. His manners were dependable; the stage was set for his first point. It was already the third week of the grouse season, and he had not tied it together.

I expected him to be a little wide and reckless, and he had certainly met those expectations. We were headed toward a woodcock area. Woodcock are good things to train young dogs and beginning hunters. They are quite tolerant of clumsy approaches and poor wingshooting technique.

I directed my companions down a side trail. It would parallel the area I intended to work. The doodles were there; the wind was in my face. The rest was up to Beans. He was very good at checking back, but his range was a little too far for the leaves and brush. I stayed off the whistle and did not yell. He already knew where I was; no sense in confirming it for him.

"Just one point, let me kill the bird, and then have him bring it back!" I thought. The plan seemed simple enough, just climb Mount Everest, turn around, and come back.

The mind wanders, along with the feet. I was busy trying to work out some background music for my thoughts when I noticed that Beans had failed to check back. Even more, there was a bird dog on point up ahead, and it looked somewhat like my heedless pup.

Could that be Beans? Tail erect, left front leg lifted, muscles taut from head to toe. Where's the goofy, gangly puppy?

I walked on the trail behind and past him, then, turned and came in from his right side. The shot was likely to be from left to right and thus against the grain for a right-handed shooter like me, but I wanted Beans to be aware of my location.

"Got to stop, boy; the angle is going bad for shooting in the brush." As soon as I halted, the bird flushed. It was a grouse.

Well, you can finish the story. If it hadn't worked out perfectly I wouldn't be telling it. Beans made plenty of mistakes afterward and still does. But I knew the right stuff was in him. The tie that binds dog to bird, bird to its cover, and me to this place.

You like to see your kid tie it all together, too. Tessa had already killed her first grouse almost three years before the October afternoon that put us on the trail next to the pond. I had her all to myself for half a day. It had snowed the day before, but the sun had returned and only patches were left in the sheltered areas. She had a Franchi 20-gauge automatic and knew how to use it. I teach all my kids how to shoot, but Tessa had taken to it. She had a natural ability that I don't think I had at the same age. The little 20-gauge semi-auto was just the right length and was bored wide open. Tessa had already proved that it was lethal.

This was in the years before Beans, when Salty and Jet were in their prime. We rested at the junction of the pond trail and the trail to my old maple deer stand. We were going to step across the creek and then follow the path around the end of the pond to the property fence. There is a heavy growth of gray dogwood between the creek and the fence, and the lack of birds on the trail indicated the berry bushes might be productive.

I led the way and we walked—single file—up the side of the hill, around a corner, and finally to the clump of bushes. Salty was making sense of it and found a grouse hiding back in the undergrowth. I could just make out the line of the dog's back and the plume of her tail. Still on one knee I gestured to Tessa that we had a point. She nodded and stood clear of the bushes.

Jet was standing next to Salty. It was partly good manners and partly intimidation by the little setter.

There was no way in for me, except to crawl, but I could send the dog.

"Jet, get 'im!"

She lived up to her name. The grouse had to jump and almost didn't make the brush tops. I can still see the bird, climbing, the feathers under its chin a light beige, the dark cover of its wings flashing to white and then back to dark as it stretched to reach the open air over Tessa.

"*Crack!*" the little 20-gauge barked. A puff of feathers lingered in the air where the bird used to be. The grouse dropped, loose and broken, into the brush on the other side of the trail. Jet snuffled it out of the bushes, and I handed it to her, bowing deeply.

"A fine shot; the best yet," I said.

"Yeah, yeah," she answered, giving that two-note rise and fall of her voice. "That was all right!"

Salty was still on point.

"Oh-oh, there's more in there." I directed Tessa to a spot a little farther down the trail.

"Stand by that log. I'm going to have to work my way into the tangle."

Tessa nodded and slipped a new shell into the magazine.

"The kid's good," I thought. "Very heads-up."

It wasn't long. Salty relocated once, and again, then locked down. Jet was standing next to Tessa. Two more grouse rattled their wings against the dogwood branches and were on the way.

One of the two made the mistake of crossing over the trail and died in the same manner as its covey mate.

"Two for two. Pretty hot shooting, Tessa!"

We didn't hit the next group until we had walked the entire north boundary. Even then, they flushed early in a scattered rise of four and then two more.

I was going to tell Tessa to split off and follow up the last pair. She was already doing it, Jet tagging along. I turned back to look for Salty, and the 20-gauge barked again. Number three was flopping back in the Labrador's mouth.

"Leave some for me!" I shouted. Tessa just waved back happily.

The way to finish the west side of the Promised Land is to walk south along a wet swamp, sending the dogs into the grass and brush. This is hard ground for finding points, but it's good hunting for a flushing dog. Salty was working for the boss, but Jet had found a new mission.

The Lab pushed and scuffled through the lumped-up mess until she struck and launched the fourth grouse up and into a quick snapshot. Not mine, Tessa's. Four up and four down.

"One more," she said holding her gloved hand up and extending the trigger finger slowly.

It was not to be, however. We did get a final flush before stepping into the hay field, but it was a poor opportunity.

Tessa shot, but the bird didn't fall. She was shocked. It was supposed to tumble.

"You know when you are getting good?" I asked.

"No," she shook her head.

"When you expect them all to fall."

She still expects them all to fall. Most of the time they do, especially in this cover. She is bound to it by the tie that comes with success.

The sweetest success belongs to my son, Max. He killed his first grouse here. I killed my first in the falling light of a dark, overcast evening, not too many miles from here. A lightning stroke of heavy No. 6 shot from the full-choke barrel of my long Remington pump gun. A road bird taken from the side of a tote trail. Tessa took hers out of a tree in a cover only half a mile from the Maple Hill Lutheran Church.

To be sure, Max had been with me from an early age, walking behind and watching. He just never had one of those golden opportunities. Even when he got older, passed his firearm-safety test, and carried a gun, the chances were never in his favor. There was so much to learn. If a bird treed, it just would not linger long enough for him to get close. If it flushed wild or even off a point, his shot—if he got one off at all—was not true.

There is a scraggly tree just to the left of the creek, where the beaver pond has watered the brush and foliage into a thick mess. It is still there. Max and I had just stepped across the rivulet when Beans pointed into the knitted tangle. I waved Max up beside me, and, true to his luck, two grouse flushed out on the opposite side—neither offering a shot.

"Damn!" I hissed. "Wait a minute! That last one just treed! C'mon Max. You still have a chance!"

The bird stayed, posed on a limb, backlit against the late-afternoon sky.

"Okay, there it is," I said, pointing with my shotgun.

"Just this one time," I thought, "give the kid a break. He has put in his miles; give him a memory!"

Max stepped around me and started to raise his gun, when a second bird, hidden in the grass, took off from under the tree-sitter.

The gun was up, Max fired, and the flushed grouse tumbled.

My son turned to look at me. "Did I get him?"

"Yes, you did, and Beans will have him back here in a moment."

"WOW!" he yelled. "He was there and then he wasn't. I can't believe I did that!"

True to his job, Beans returned the grouse, a little soggy from its fall into the swamp but gorgeous to a boy who had just made the impossible become possible.

Small wonder, then, that I have a soft squeeze in my heart when I sit watching the sun set out here. I am as bound to the four corners of this land as a musician is to his sheet music. My experiences here have accumulated to the point where this is not a long string of separate memories. They have piled up and attained a certain mass. Now, the Promised Land has become more than just days spent hunting. All of it has melted together to become this place.

Blest be this tie that binds.

CHAPTER ELEVEN
A Full Count

Children don't come with instruction books. I have three kids, and I lost another. So, while I can demonstrate time on the job and a full spectrum of experience—from joy to despair—over twenty-five years, the best I can say on the subject is that perfection has eluded me. I sometimes question whether I am even competent to raise them. They all seem to sit up and take nourishment, walk, talk, and perform daily functions without my help. But I can't say that when I have set any of them off in a particular direction, they have stayed the course I wanted them to follow.

I guess kids are like those small sailboats I used to see in park ponds. Some were well made; some were just boards and sticks. But each one pushed off to go in one way and, blown around, went in another. My boats were of my design but were on their way without me, the winds of fate for their fuel.

I have set two of my three children on the hunter's road. I have one left. You'd   think that after two tries I would have gained some idea of how to go about making a bird hunter out of the third in an easy and seamless fashion. But it does not work that way. Every time I trained a child I was in a different part of my life. And, every child presents a different bunch of raw material. My first, Tessa, was my spitting image in a girl. The next was my son, Max. The last is Molly, her dark-haired mother in miniature.

I was once around a campfire when the topic turned from the results of the day to women. One of our number was, in physical terms and by his own good-natured admission, "looks impaired." On the other hand, his wife was a vision of beauty and grace. His daughters were already contest winners.

"Orville," one fellow asked, "how did an ugly dog like you make those beautiful daughters?"

"Easy," he replied, "I had the pattern right in front of me."

It follows, then, that the job of forming a bird hunter from my own stock could be done by drawing upon the remembered efforts of my father, to which process I could add those child-hood experiences and my present knowledge.

That's a great theory, but it doesn't work well.

When I was about twelve my father put a gun in my hands. In my family the first gun was preceded by many years of expo-sure to the musty woolens and smoky conversation of deer hunters. The World War II generation. The hard-living, any-thing-is-possible-so-let's-go-to-the-moon people. A far cry from our cautious, low-fat, mandatory-helmet-wearing, seatbelt-strapped generation. I see their faces beaming with youth and promise in pictures of hunting camps, their arms around each other, grinning through the blue smoke of unfiltered cigarettes, wearing wool hats (cocked to one side or the other) and plaid clothes, hoisting Hamms beer to the camera. Dad was a deer hunter. So was my brother and, therefore, so was I. Walking between the trees for grouse came a while later.

My bird-hunting seed took root in the passenger seat of a 1947 Willys Jeep. If grouse were to be killed in any place other than the clear rut of a two-track country road, I didn't know about it. I thought that was where the bird was born, prospered, and died. It never occurred to me, or to anyone else of my acquaintance, that the "partridge" could be found anyplace else. There were rumors, to be sure, but the stories in sports magazines were as suspect as the advice any hired writer put between the covers of a picture book. Deer lived in the woods, ducks on the water, and game birds on tote roads.

That whole culture is gone. I clearly recall no fewer than five black or dark blue cars, each one following the other down a country road. Every driver had a Camel cigarette dangling from his lip, and every passenger seat had a kid with a long-barreled duck gun stuck in a canvas case between his legs. That was called "partridge hunting," and that, boy, is how it was done! ("Yessir, I'll keep watching.") On the other hand, cable TV presents my kids with a different icon. The positive display of fair chase is a nice change, but now we have a fellow wearing seven kinds of camouflage, with the sound of the South in his voice or a sport-utility-driving, Martha-Stewart-goes-bird-hunting format. This guy is complete with stylish English setter, spotless field wear, and matching safari hat.

Therefore, if the best instruction is to lead by example, my first two kids have followed a blueprint that is best described as a somewhat tattered and rumpled guide. This is a fact made apparent to me when, after a long wait, I was invited to a hunt as a celebrity writer. I turned out the next morning in my full bird-shooting garb. It was stained, patched canvas trousers tucked into boot socks; off-green suspenders over a well-rubbed, but clean, white shirt; and a rime-stained, orange baseball cap. I shook hands with a nearby group of catalog models, and the first question was:

"Are you the guide?"

The experience I gained with the first of my children should have been helpful for the second. The first Lundrigan to start bird hunting was Tessa. I had no idea how to go about this in the proper way. But after hauling around a heavy 12-gauge in my early years, I knew enough to give her a light 20-gauge gun and train her how to use it safely. After that I just considered her to be sort of a miniature Ted. In those years, this was not a good thing.

The grouse cycle was at its peak; my setter, Salty, was at her peak; and I covered ground like a dog-driven coyote. I marvel now and sometime just may ask Tessa, "How did you ever keep up?" But she did. She walked down other men and never asked for, or received, quarter. I had some close calls. The brush in her face, the heat, the cold, and the frustration of lost opportunities must have been discouraging. I know now that she wanted to quit, but she never showed it to me. I know this because I was the same peerless example for my son. By this time, my wife had reached her saturation point and, like the tolerant child-raiser she is, she took me aside.

"Our kids are not you!" she said. "This is supposed to be fun, and your idea of fun is different than that of anybody I have ever known!"

This part was true. I was not my father, and I was not the new icon. On the other hand, what was I? If I wanted my two kids to be bird hunters I had to make a connection. I assumed they were like me at the same age. Once I was up and in the woods with a shotgun, my father couldn't have turned me back into the child I was before that season if he had wanted to. I had no example to be like, and I did not know anyone to watch and learn from.

So, I made more mistakes. When I was mad at the dog, I got irritable with the kids. If I missed an easy shot, I showed my anger, instead of teaching them to slough it off. As Tessa got older and her life as a university student filled up the fall week-ends, Max took her place. Of the two, he got it the worst, because I think I saw him as a little me, only without the defects that I allow myself.

Fathers and sons are a whole new world. I could temper my ambition with Tessa because she always exceeded what I thought she, as a girl, could do. She also had—and still has—the style. An actress on television or in a movie picks up a shotgun and handles it as if it smells bad and is likely to catch fire. Tessa handles her Franchi 20-gauge auto as if she was born with it. She walks in on a point with a sure and steady step, not tentative but direct. The dogs love her.

Max never reminded me of myself or, in the words of my mother: "You mean the way you remember yourself."

There are so many things I would do differently now. We needed to laugh more. But at that time in my bird shooting life, I didn't see much about it that was funny. Dogs were to perform well, birds were to fall when shot at, ground was there to be covered, and fifty flushes in a day was about right. I needed to divide my time and share the season in two ways. First to take one day to hunt hard, pursue, and excel on my own; then, to back off, turn down the fire, and spend the next day with Tessa or Max at a lower and slower pace. Max was, and is, a willing student but he likes to look at the big picture, not just a small part of it. A day in the Promised Land or on Mayo Creek was, and is, full of things to see and do.

We were after two grouse. They lived in the Promised Land's west swamp, a long stretch of wet grass and alders with clumps of berries. The first two points had been productive, but the pair had stayed ahead of the dog in low alders. I stayed with Beans, stepping over deadfalls and sliding under bent branches. The dog, in turn, pushed the birds—but not too hard. They were running and he, in his way, was stopping to point, then going ahead when I came alongside. Max was off to the right, or maybe the left, but was somewhere . . . around. Hot running, man and dog got to the end of the alders, then ducked under a fallen oak, and in twenty more steps the birds huddled down for the last rise.

Where's Max? Here is his chance, and he is going to miss out! These two won't hold for long. They didn't, either. One came up and I shot it down; the second jumped up at the shot and suffered the same fate. Two up, two down—over a solid point. Now that is an example to follow. Suddenly, Max was there.

He walked to me, extended his hand and put it on my right arm.

"Dad," he implored, "can't you just slow down?"

Yes, of course I could. Max got a short lecture in the value of speed and, a half hour later when the importance of it struck me, an apology for my being just slightly brighter than our German shorthair. But the memory was made.

So, I have let two go by, and Molly is left. I want some redemption. I am willing to be saved. Yes, my instinct tells me, just as long as your salvation leaves your individual whims and passions in place. And, so it was that this year, Molly, the youngest and most like her mother, asked to go along.

"I can do this," I told her mother, Cheryl.

She looked to the left and right. I had dug up some old nylon-faced pants from Tessa's younger days, and had removed the felt liners from last year's winter boots. Molly had grown some, and these boots would be just right with heavy socks. Cheryl wanted to be sure Molly was busy putting on her new (old) hunting clothes before speaking.

A straight, hard finger poked me in the chest. "Just remember, it is supposed to be FUN!"

"It will be, I have the lunch all ready for the grill, we are going to the Promised Land, the trails are cut, it is sunny and mild. I'll be good; I promise." (Honest, Mom.)

There was hope for redemption, even cause for it. Beans had been bred to a lovely lady shorthair and the bony, strapping, big-footed result of the union was before me in the form of Butch, son of Beans. Actually that would be spelled "Buche" since he's German, you know. Cheryl had seen how slack I was with Butch, in comparison to the other bird dogs over the years. The boy was almost pure white, with his father's square, brown head. He was affable, likeable, and a huge chip off his daddy's block. More to the point, Molly adored him and his welfare was her concern.

The bird population was in its ten-year low cycle. While I hoped for some action, I was more concerned with Molly having a good time. She had seen me work the dogs in the yard, but this was her first hunt. It was very quiet, but nice in its own way.

We made a long walk down the east side along the pond, then around the corner to the very spot where Max had shot his first grouse. I was about to point this out to Molly when I got inter-rupted. Beans was locked up in an intense point, backed by his son, Butch. It was tailor-made. Molly could see it all, I was about to become the hero, her first memory of bird hunting would be her father walking in on a grouse pointed by both of the dogs. It would fall in a puff of feathers and be retrieved to hand.

The grouse flushed up, showing itself perfectly in a backlit opening. I missed. Startled by the shot, the bird flattened out a bit, turning slightly to the right. I missed a second time.

There is no greater punishment than having to serve as a good example. Stunned, speechless by virtue of my daughter being present, I had to absorb this incredible event. Then I had to swallow it, turn to her, and say, "Oh, shoot, I missed."

"It's okay, Daddy, you'll get the next one."

I was even a little light-headed. I wondered whether I would need a paper bag to breath into. Gathering what little remained of my ego and dignity, I followed the dogs uphill, where they promptly—and jointly—pointed again.

The little gods have a sense of humor, I thought, I can hear them twittering in the delight of this moment. "Molly, look. Beans and Butch are on point again."

I was going into a mental rehearsal of just how to pull off the shot when an out-of-season woodcock rose up from in front of the two dogs. "Thank you, for that," I thought. "I am in no condition to go through it again."

The walk continued over the ridge and down into the creek valley. Molly had found a piece of brush with a punky center and was busy picking out the soft fiber with another small stick.

The lesser gods have mercy, and to prove it they arranged a short flashy point by Beans that flushed two gray-tailed fast-movers from low left, across the stream, one after the other. The lead bird fell in a heap, and Molly hollered, "Got him!"

I didn't chance a second shot.

We took some rest stops on my favorite logs. Important things were discussed—like whether bugs sleep. (I don't know.) And whether grouse smell good because they don't seem to have any smell at all. (Dogs like them.)

We stayed out of the brush, collected some red and yellow leaves, and watched the dogs point two squirrels—and something else that simply walked away.

"How can it be a false point?" she asked. "Butchy just might be right."

"We'll never know, for sure, but his daddy and your daddy think he's goofing off."

It is just my opinion, but I think fewer kids are hunting these days. Those times I spent in the seat of an old car were not the same experience that my own children had. Some of what I did with them was good, and most was better than riding the dusty roads of the late 1950s. The electronic world offers pretty stout competition at considerably less effort. I think the hunting gene is still in there. In spite of all that the media tries to do to purge it or shame it into submission, it will rise to the top. Not every child will catch the opportunity to light up this small part of their double helix, and not every child that has the chance will come away with a positive experience. The important thing is to create the opportunity. Even if we screw it up, it will probably come to some good.

CHAPTER TWELVE
Waltzes with Wild Things

I have gotten down on my hands and knees and looked, carefully, above Beans's head. I have never seen a dark cloud hovering there. Yet, in his eight years as my third companion bird dog, Beans has been sprayed four times by skunks in no less than seven encounters. He has a history with skunks. I hunted my setter, Salty, and two Labrador retrievers for over twenty years and never had an incident. Beans just seems to like skunks. Once is enough, twice is bad luck, but more than three times begins to look like personal preference.

The worst, by far, was on the grassy edge of a ditch in far northwestern Minnesota. He and I were rookie sharptail-grouse hunters, poking along a drain under the false impression that we knew what we were doing. He pointed, solid and firm. Expecting the first flush of my first sharptail, I walked up alongside him. The bluestem was thick; I could see nothing. After a few kicks into the broom sedge I stepped back to look for a better way.

Beans leaned forward, sticking his nose down into the matted wall. Then, he leaped backward, yelping in surprise. Hanging on his lower lip, like a black-and-white Christmas tree ornament, was a skunk!

The little polecat had sunk its teeth into his jowl and was swinging back and forth, spraying every square inch of my hapless dog like a punctured gas bag. Beans tossed his head and danced in panic. I shouted; it was the only thing I could do.

"Beans! Let go! Let go!"

He would have if he could have. But, his was not the "let" to "go." He was the critter being bitten, not the biter. After a few more good passes, the skunk dropped off. I scored on the only item of wild anything I was to see that day.

When a skunk gets its work done really well, there is no odor of "skunk." There is, instead, a chemical taste, a burning of the eyes. The nose is completely overwhelmed. Beans had not been "sprayed"; he had been painted, dipped, soaked, and immersed in polecat oil.

Friends, it is a true thing, and I tell it to you now. There is nothing—not one thing, save outright skinning—that will move this substance to another place. I had one saving grace (from a benevolent and all-seeing God). I own a pickup truck, and the back of it has a camper top. We went home; Beans was in the back and I was in the cab with the windows up and the music on. Let you owners of enclosed sport-utility vehicles take note. Although the passage of time, several applications of "Skunk-Off," several baths with super detergent Tide, and harsh scrubbing just made the old boy tolerable, he did not learn.

The original makers of my little Westley Richards 20-gauge double grouse gun did not foresee this application, but I killed six more skunks near Beans while defending him. I shot them from behind while they sighted in on his perfect point. I shot them after the fact. I even shot one that was trying to sneak up on him from behind. I submit that the little bird gun's current record of seven skunk kills certainly makes me an "ace" and quite possibly sets a world mark for a gun of this impeccable breeding. I further suspect the original designers of my German shorthair rush to be seated alongside our divine Master, and when all look down on the two of us, they must from time to time poke each other in the ribs and say: "There he goes again, only this time it's a wolf!"

Wolves are back, and whether you agree with me or not, I can tell you from my own personal experience that they no longer fear man. A timber wolf is a whole world apart from the pointy-nosed little coyotes that occasionally come out to see me.

True to form, Beans had made a cast into a birdy-looking piece of brush adjacent to a grassy slough. It was a wild piece of country but nothing extraordinary. The corner he was searching was right next to a cattle pasture. Suddenly, the dog's bell started ringing wildly. He was fleeing for his life. When in danger or in doubt, Beans runs to me, bringing along whatever he is waltzing with. This time it was an enormous gray wolf.

The dog was going full speed, and he is not a slow runner. The wolf was just loping along. When Beans got within twenty feet or so of me, the beast turned his head to the side and extended his neck. From my view he intended to hamstring the dog. I hollered "Wolf, hey, wolf!" and fired my 20-gauge into the ground in front of him. He stopped. He stared, and I stared back. He returned my gaze, eye for eye. I knew two things: first, that he was not afraid and second, that the 20-gauge was not big enough.

The wolf then walked off. He didn't duck and run; he just walked, tail straight out, ambling back into the woods. I never got an answer to what that was all about. Instead, Beans moved on to bigger, badder things.

Sometimes you eat the bear, and sometimes he eats you—a favorite homily of mine and not a bad epitaph for a gravestone. I've used it many times to sum up a streak of hard luck. Others might call it buzzard luck, but I like eating the bear, or vice versa. The image gives bad luck some balance.

I would never want to shoot a bear. The common practice is to fill pails with grease, old bakery goods, and various other concoctions of goodies, then climb up a nearby tree and wait. It must be a lot like shooting your favorite Labrador retriever over its food bowl. I understand the reason for the bait. One on one, a bear in the woods is more than a match for a foot hunter. If that were not so, I would have seen many more.

I have now seen one, up close and personal. I assure you, once is enough.

After almost fifteen years of bird hunting on the Promised Land, I sold my big poplars on the west side to the Richards

Brothers Logging Company. Some of the covers had grown a little long in the tooth to support a good population of grouse.

A dense seepage adjoined my new clear-cut. Already the suckers of new poplar were waving their big green leaves between low-cut stumps. A green foreground nodding in front of a living wall. Son Max and I had watched a solid point by Beans and had flushed a covey of six grouse, mostly young birds. I had taken one, and the rest had scattered away. Some had flown toward the dense regrowth.

At first, I merely noticed a heavy, musky odor lingering around the area. It wasn't exactly skunk. The smell was like dirty clothes—a greasy, sweat stink. I had smelled it before; there are lots of odors in the woods. Most of the time this particular smell was somewhere in the area of a porcupine. I had killed two porcupines pointed by Beans, and I was thankful for their slow speed. Skunks were bad habit enough. If Beans was slapped up in a dance with a porcupine, it would be consistent with his brand of luck.

"Smell that?" I asked Max.

"Yeah, what is it?" he answered.

"I think it's a porcupine—not sharp enough for old skunk spray," I said.

"Something needs a bath." Max was right; it was foul body odor.

"Where's Beans?" I asked. Max serves as my hearing aide. While the dog bell has a good middle tone, the years have progressed and I find that my range is decreasing.

"He's over there." Max pointed to the wall of poplar saplings in the seepage.

"Let's bring him in; I don't want him to get into a porcupine."

I had just lifted my whistle to my mouth when it started.

Beans was barking, then baying like a hound.

"Oh, oh," I said. "Let's get going; he's got a porky!"

Max and I ran down the trail to the green wall. We looked for a way in.

"There's a deer trail!" I said. I led and Max followed close behind. The tone of the barking changed to a high panic.

"Beans! Come!" I yelled. He must have heard me because his bell was getting louder, heading right toward us. Then there was another sound. Heavy footfalls.

"What's this?" I thought, "A cow or even a bull coming?"

Beans rounded a corner and zipped by us. In the narrow poplar hallway, he was going flat out, as hard as his muscles could pour it on, followed closely by a bear!

Three impressions remain with me today and will, I suspect, for the rest of my life: Big! Round! Black!

And, there are three smaller details: a wet black nose with a brown circle around it and two bright black eyes. It was not an animal shape. Head on, a bear is a deep, dark ball.

I yelled "Hey! Hey!" and waved my arms. The bear hit the brakes.

Almost simultaneously I turned to Max: "Max! Bear! Run!"

I turned back to the black ball, thinking that a 20-gauge side-by-side is very small. We spent one of those three-heartbeat eternities, then—mutually—agreed to run opposite ways. I made the main trail in a few long strides. Max was standing on it with his gun up, covering my exit from the woods.

We stood together, panting.

He looked at me. "Bear," he said.

I looked at him. "Yeah, Bear."

"What was that all about?" It was a question not addressed for an answer but just the first thing in my mind.

Beans came back up the trail, his whole body shaking, very happy to see us. He had the answer but wasn't talking.

"Will the bear come back?" Max asked.

"No, but I think we will leave that place alone for today."

Some dogs, in the exercise of their free will, are lightning rods for hard luck. Beans seems to be like that. If it is the way of God to watch over the affairs of men and bird dogs, and if it is true that He weeps over what He sees, then likewise, I think He must have the capacity to be amused. Knowing full well in his infinite wisdom how things are going to turn out, He must on occasion turn to the angels of deceased German-shorthair breeders and say, "Did you see THAT?"

The presence of a bear in my grouse covers was an element I'd never had to deal with. Until this incident, a bear was like foxfire, often reported but seldom seen. Was it a chance event, or were we going to have problems?

Two weeks passed. Max and I returned to the Promised Land, the bear incident fresh in our minds but set aside.

When Max started hunting with me I wanted him to be able to keep in touch. It is easy to get separated or turned around. I bought two small pocket radios. We would turn them on and then, from time to time, check up if we didn't see or hear one another. And so it was on this day.

"Max, you hunt down the fence line," I said. "I'm going to walk along the edge of the heavy poplar, and I'll meet you where it comes up to the fence." Roughly speaking, he would be on one side of the place where the bear had chased Beans, and I would be on the other.

Beans stayed with me, and I worked the edge of the trail. In about twenty minutes my radio crackled alive.

"Bear! Bear!" said Max's voice.

"Easy, easy. Where are you?"

"On the fence. There goes a big one and one, two, three little ones!"

"Are you okay?" I asked.

"Yeah, just a little scared. The big one jumped the fence, and the three little ones went underneath."

That was the answer to the question. Two weeks ago Beans must have chased the cubs and then run up against momma. She was hot on his tail when Max and I came along. In the course of today's business, she was glad to run out the back side.

"Okay, just keep coming, Max. Sing a little," I said.

I never saw the bear again. I poked around in the area after freeze-up. The stumps and logs were torn up and turned over. She was probably holed up under one of the big slash piles that I had made. The cubs would be leaving in the spring; as far as I was concerned the old girl was welcome to stay or leave.

After seven skunks, two porcupines, a timber wolf, and a bear, that should have been it. How much bad luck can one dog have? It's not as if wild things had a meeting and declared my German shorthair an undesirable alien.

No, they had a meeting and declared that this pup would inherit the title of *Things That Tick Us Off*.

I knew nothing about it. Two years had gone by without a skunk bath or a face-to-face incident with anything more fearsome than a red squirrel. Beans had created his successor, the affable and loose-jointed clone we named Butch. It was Butch's first year; I didn't expect much from him. I just wanted him to have a good time, get crazy about grouse, and mimic his old man.

He could do that. He ran like Beans, hunted like him, watched everything the old boy did, and carried it at least one step further. He was bigger, faster, and stronger. Whatever else it is that stirs up God's toothy creatures, he had also. In abundance.

Beans, Butch, and I had crossed the road from the Promised Land into the Gravley South covert. The little creek that feeds our beaver pond travels through this mixed-hardwood river bottom. There is almost always a covey of grouse that grows up on the opposite side of the creek. Now that the beaver have dammed the flow, there is a lot more water to get around, but a low-water ford makes up the shallow end, and we crossed there.

The covey was occupied elsewhere that late morning. I brought the boys back through the middle of the woodlot by using a well-worn pasture trail. Beans trotted alongside; Butch was off to the right in the woods.

There was no mistake about it. The snarls, howls, barking, and yelps meant Butch had just been crowned successor to his father's fortune. It could not have been otherwise because Beans was standing right by my side.

What a row! I started to trot toward the noise, anxious about what I was going to find when I got there and wishing that the little Westley was a .416 Rigby, given the history of these encounters. Within a moment a large, long animal hopped out on the trail and stopped. It was an otter, full grown, splendid in black, and at least forty or fifty pounds. It growled at us. The howls and yelps continued in the background. This was not good. Butch must be tied up with another otter, I thought, and he was no match for it.

I raised the shotgun and Beans stepped forward, returning the growl and making ready to get between us. The big otter backed away and flowed down the trail, snakelike in its hump-backed gait. We turned back toward the woods.

It reminded me of those old western movies, where two cowboys come rolling out of a bar and into the street. Butch and the otter tumbled out of the brush, over and over, first one on top and then the other. I hollered at Butch to break it off, and the two came apart. This was a young otter the size of a big cat. Butch promptly jumped back on it and gave it a hard shake. The otter spun around in his jaws and clawed his nose. Startled, the dog dropped the animal. But the otter had only just begun to fight.

It was back at Butch in a jump, and even though the dog was now in full retreat, the young otter pressed its attack, pushing him down the trail toward the beaver water. Beans jumped in from our side. Unsportsmanlike, for sure, but this was not a tag-team event. The otter was more than game for it. It split Beans's ear, then rolled him over. Suddenly, both of them were backing up.

The whole event had a screaming, yelling, cursing background, complete with a blowing whistle. I wanted to call a time-out or perhaps a personal foul. Anything to save my dogs from about twenty pounds of pure malice.

I could have fired into the air, but at the time I wanted to shoot the otter and could not get an opening. That spitfire had both dogs backing up as fast as they could go and was between us. Neither dog dared to turn around, and I wasn't going to jump in front for fear of those snapping jaws and raking claws.

It was not until both Beans and Butch were standing in the

flowage that the otter backed off the offensive and smoothly swam away. I sat down, hoarse from screaming. Butch stood in the water, his nose dripping blood, and Beans did likewise, crimson running from his left ear flap.

"Well, and let that be a lesson to you," I said to them.

But, on reflection, I think that it was just more of the same being passed to the next generation. Because two weeks later Butch led me out of the woods, and there was a full-grown coyote waiting for him at my truck! A bob-and-weave standoff continued until I ran close enough to burn the brush wolf with two loads of bird shot.

There used to be a character named Joe Doaks in a movie short. I believe the series was called *Behind the Eight Ball*. Anyway, whenever Joe walked by an attractive woman, she would haul off and slap him, then declare, "You remind me of someone I hate!"

It must be like that for my boys, and until I get a release from those heavenly German dog breeders, I think my bird hunting will be interrupted from time to time by waltzes with wild things.

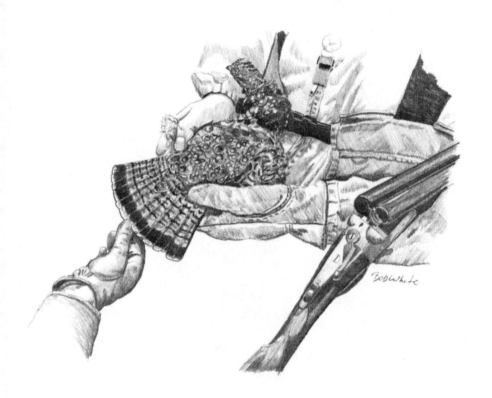

CHAPTER THIRTEEN
A Gentleman's Sport

"Who *are* those guys?"

It's a favorite line from the movie about Butch Cassidy and the Sundance Kid. They are running from a posse of railroad detectives and, as their tricks fail, the lawmen track Butch and Sundance across desert, shale slopes, and solid rock. Butch crawls to the edge of the rock cliff, amazed, and asks, "Who *are* those guys?"

My friend Bill and I chased a grouse in that same way one late afternoon into early evening. This one bird required four points, five flushes, twelve shots, and three hits to finally bring him down. The grouse caused Mike McIntosh to twist his knee on the first rise and Bill Habein to fall flat and cut open his face on the second. As for me, I got off easy. I sank up to my hips in a black-mud bog.

Still, though Butch and Sundance got away, the "Kevlar" grouse did not.

*   *   *

The old town road leaves the highway and runs, straight as a string, past the back of the Promised Land, to where a wind-faded old house once stood. Local lore had it that the place used to be a beer joint, card parlor, and speakeasy. The son of the people who lived there said that was not true, but no matter; it's gone now.

Bill and I used to drive to the end of the road and park in the yard of the old place to hunt the edge of a big swamp about another half-mile across rocky, open ground. In the whole forty acres between the house and the swamp, there was only one tree, growing out of the middle of a rockpile.

It was the end of a bright and happy afternoon. Bill and I walked to the trucks, glad for the open ground after a day spent in close company with alder brush. We had a few birds, my little white setter had worked very well, and as if to prove she still had energy left, Salty ran on ahead, stopping at the lone tree.

"What's she rolling in?" Bill asked.

"Hmmm. She never has dipped into cow pies, and there's no cattle out here. I don't know—just dust and dirt," I guessed.

We drew closer. The setter's immaculate white coat was streaked with something dark. Then the vapor hit me. "Awwww, that's rotten! What is it?"

I ran to the base of the tree. There lay the squished flat, rancid, rotted remains of a northern pike. Some fish hawk had carried it into the tree to eat and had not dined nearly well enough.

My cultured, well-mannered, and pedigreed dog had dipped her shoulder into this mess and rolled in ecstasy. It took my breath away. Literally. I had to breathe through my mouth to get close enough to drag her away.

His eyes brimming with tears of laughter, Bill said, "Good breeding will out."

The only water was the stream that feeds my Promised Land pond waters as it runs across the road from its course through the adjoining covert. The culvert was filled by the beavers long ago, and the township—tired of trying to keep it open—simply quit. Oliver Gravely, tired of bugging officials to keep the culvert open, dumped several loads of crushed rock there to make a crossing good enough for trucks and tractors going along the road and to prevent water from going across it. I dunked the bony white dog into the puddles and rubbed her down with sand and grass.

"Some people pay good money for this stuff," I said to Bill. "They call it compost tea water. I think you're missing out on a real horticultural bargain."

Just up the hill, toward the highway, was the wooded pasture owned by the same Oliver Gravley. He's gone now, but he was generous with his land. I called this place "Gravley South" for two reasons. First, it was south of the Promised Land and, second, the name implied a hospitality of fine breeding, good manners, and old plantations.

Large oaks and stately maples grew among clumps of berry bushes on the side closest to the road. The waterway that I was using as my dog bath flowed from a valley that it had eroded over

the years. This little stream, with patience and without the inter-
ference of beavers, started somewhere beyond Oliver's fences and
bent its way across an open grass prairie in the middle of the
wooded pasture. When it reached the tree groves making up the
woods, it widened and divided the country into two pieces of
woods separated by a brush-filled backwater.

On one side of the backwater the trees had been selectively
cut for saw logs at one time, causing small openings that had
grown back in poplar saplings. Like the woods on the Promised
Land side of the road, this area had trails bulldozed through it.
Oliver used his bulldozer to wander wherever Oliver wanted to
go. It was different on the town-road side, however, because the
cattle kept the trails mowed down, and the isolated oaks and
maples were very old. The light was more diffused, and the
whole place had the look of an aged sporting print. All that was
necessary to make it into a shooting estate was Spanish moss
and stone walls.

The dog laundry was almost done. A sand-scrubbed setter is
not a pretty thing to see. Quite a bit of the fish sauce and the tea
created by its mixture in the stream had found its way onto me,
as well. I stood up and let the dog shake off.

"I wish I had a picture of this," said Bill. "It wouldn't make
the *Gentleman's Hunting Quarterly* but I'll bet I could get into the
Sewer Suckers News."

Fine clothes, broad-brimmed hats, and a coordinated appearance have their place, of course, and Gravely South is that place.
It has its dense corners, but open shots can be expected on occa-

sion. It is, in most ways, a place where a grouse hunter might believe it is possible to hunt "pa'tridge" with a tie and tweeds. Mike McIntosh came close to that gentility once. He shot a high-flying bird in here with his 28-gauge.

I watched it very carefully until its glide took it out of sight on the Promised Land side of the road. The grouse had not showed any signs of a hit, but its flight line was so obvious that I was sure my dog could find it for a reflush. The truck was parked over there anyway, and we were on the return trip. Mike and I crossed the road, reset the flight line on that side, and ran the dog through the closest dense corner, twice. Nothing came out. We gave up and walked to the truck, both of us agreeing that the bird had looked easy to find but apparently went farther than we thought. We did not take into account the good manners of Gravely South. The high-flying grouse lay stone dead on the hard dirt driveway of the field road, wings spread out, head curled under its breast, just in front of my vehicle.

So it was on another golden October afternoon, when Bill Habein and Ted Lundrigan came with their good friend Michael McIntosh to hunt grouse at Gravley South in the genteel fashion of world sportsmen. It should be said that Michael's knee and our other various joints were creaky from the two previous days of "rough shooting" (damn rough), and we were looking for a break. With the anticipation of some easy and well-mannered grouse, we three set off. I carried my Parker 12-bore, Bill had his W.C. Scott 12-bore, and Michael brought his John Wilkes 12. Mike probably had some tweeds but not with him. It was more a three-way mutual frame of mind, a belief in the possibilities portrayed in classic shooting literature. Unfortunately, the grouse were not on the same page.

The birds flushed openly as described. They just did it at great distance and not in large numbers. With the sun resting on the treetops, we had only our gentlemanly attitude for a reward.

"Bad form! They won't hold for a point." I said.

"I'd even take a poor shot, pointed or not," said Bill.

"We're going to have to cut me a crutch," spoke Michael.

I took the inside of the creek, with the dog. Bill took the outside next to the woods, and Mike covered the open alley. We intended to make one last pass through an open glade of young poplar, following the waterway to the property boundary.

I heard the bird flush wild on my left, somewhere in the vicinity of Mike. One shot and a shout: "*Bang!* Owwww!" I hustled through the young trees, meeting Bill coming from the other way.

"Did you shoot?" I asked.

"No, did you?" Bill replied. I shook my head.

Mike was standing—a good sign—but holding on to a poplar sapling with his left hand, his gun open and in the crook of his right arm. "That grouse got up right *next* to me! I turned to get at him and twisted my sore knee."

"Do you want to sit down?" I asked.

"No, if I did that I'd be here all fall and winter. Let's find a strong limb to use as a walking stick, and I'll hobble back to the trucks. I hit him, though—knocked off the far side of his tail."

Bill came back with a dry, straight stick and two tail feathers.

"Did he fly toward the fence?" he asked. Mike nodded his head, took the stick, and balanced his shotgun on his shoulder.

"We'll go after the bird. You start for the trucks. Meet you there," I said.

"Think he'll be okay?" Bill asked, closing his gun.

"He's Scottish, he's used to dealing with loss; it's success he can't stand," I said. We both laughed, and I whistled up Salty. Time was getting short, and the shadows were getting long.

Just within earshot, a grouse with half his tail shot away hustled under a bush. The clump was part of a fence, growing near a bundle of old barbed wire.

Salty made two casts, one to the right, then back left, across the open strip between the poplar and the woods. When she emerged at the fence, she froze into a solid, positive point.

"There it is," I said to Bill in a low voice, "in that clump."

He nodded, and, because the point was on his side of the opening, he had the first shot. Bill was stepping past the dog, when, suddenly, he was gone! A booted leg reappeared then disappeared, and I saw his Scott shotgun bounce across the short grass. It was open, both shells spilling on the ground.

Salty closed the distance between herself and the bird, and froze. It had moved, and she had reacted to stop it.

"Bill?" I walked out of the poplar grove. He was flat out on the ground, face first. The grouse chose that moment to flush. Bill raised his head and I shot twice, sending the bird off down the fence, where it turned into the woods edge, flaring its half tail like cavalry colors.

Bill pushed himself back and pulled his leg out of a loop of old barbed wire. He had fallen hard and quickly. On the way down he had the presence of mind to thumb the top lever of the double. I handed him the Scott; its action and breech were filled with dirt and grass.

He sat back on his haunches, took out his pocket knife, and dug the dirt out of the game gun.

"Say something. Are you okay?" I asked.

He looked up into my face. "We," he said, "are going to find, flush, and *kill* that bird if it takes all night."

"You're bleeding," I answered.

"I'm what?"

"Bleeding; your right cheek is cut open," I gestured with my hand, pointing to a red stream trickling down his face.

He stood up, blew through the barrels, reloaded, and snapped the gun shut. Bill never, ever, snapped that gun shut. "Where'd that sucker go?"

"See that oak up there with the bare limb sticking out? He flew under that and flared his wings. I put him ten yards farther and slightly left."

Salty was already at the oak. The half-tailed grouse trotted under a log, jumped on top, ran its length, hopped off, and scurried behind a gray dogwood bush. It would have gone farther, but a wise little white dog was watching. The setter's head was low to the ground, peering under the leafy screen. Eye to eye, the bird stopped, then settled itself down in the leaf-covered duff to wait.

"She's got him!" I whispered. "See her tail?" Bill nodded his head. "Right on the other side of the dogwood." Bill nodded again, slowly, up and down.

We walked in, one of us on each side, guns up.

The grouse jumped off the ground, flew up over the setter, and in the instant it touched the open air next to the fence, it rolled left. The load of shot from the right barrel of Bill's gun cut the air where the bird would have been. It lost some speed in the turn and dipped as it cut in to the woods. My shot sizzled over the top, but it cut away some feathers. The grouse bored straight ahead, dodged behind a tree, its bark flying into the air from two more shots, fired simultaneously.

Salty didn't wait. She followed the grouse at a hard run.

"I burned him, but it wasn't enough," I said. "Can you see where he cut back into the woods?"

"I've got a line," Bill answered, loading as he trotted along the fence.

Battered but not defeated, the half-tailed grouse lowered its flaps and landed. It looked back. The white setter was slowing down, drawing the vapor trail into her nose. Two men trotted along behind the dog, guns ready, heads up. "Who *are* those guys?"

The dog's bell stopped. This time the grouse ran, head down, slipping between the hazel brush stems until it came to the edge of a cross trail. It stopped. The shadows were long, and the grass edge was high.

"Point!" I called in a hoarse whisper. We walked past Salty. Nothing. Bill turned out to the fence line; I turned inside. Still nothing. Salty pushed ahead, searching, her nose down on the ground.

"He's running," I called.

"I've got him," answered Bill, "over here by this old trail." No sooner had he spoken than the bird flew right at his head, then banked sharp left. The first chance was too close, and the second chance was lost in the trees. I took one long shot. Three points, four flushes, and nine shots. The bird was still going, and, so were we.

"It's hanging a leg," Bill said as I caught up to him. "Your last shot must have done some more damage."

"Did you get a line?" I asked.

"Not really," Bill closed his gun. "So far it has stayed pretty close to the edge, and Salty is up there someplace."

"Your cheek has stopped bleeding. Does it hurt?" I asked.

"Can't feel it yet, but I will tomorrow," he answered.

The grouse had landed and could run no more. It wriggled back and forth in the leaves, burying its body in the musty compost. The footfalls of the white dog went by. The grouse lifted its head; the two men were coming, straight and fast.

The dog was back, it moved its head to one side, then the other. It came close and stopped. The bird gathered its good leg under it, and rested as much weight on the sore leg as it dared.

"We've got him again. Salty says he's close—I'm guessing right in front of her. If I read her correctly the grouse can be pushed out into the open. I'll come in from the woods and slightly in front of the dog."

Bill stepped toward the fence and nodded.

Taking steady paces, measuring steps without hesitation, I drew close enough to see the top of Salty's head. I stopped suddenly, bringing my left foot to the ground hard and placing it in the direction I thought the flush would go.

Three shots rippled, each on the heels of the other. First Bill, then me, then Bill again. The grouse fell in a heap, one wing fluttering and broken. He was done. The Kevlar grouse lay in the short grass by the fence, where Bill picked it up after Salty had snuffled him.

"Four points, five flushes, and twelve shots. Who the hell *is* this bird?"

I took it from him, turning it over in my hands and smoothing its feathers. "He's not as big as I thought he'd be. I hope he doesn't represent the runt of the litter. I don't think I have enough shells to deal with the prize winners."

The sun had settled, sliding down the tree trunks halfway into the horizon. Bill and I walked back along the fence, past the open alley between the poplars, staying with the wire boundary until we reached a cow-tracked road heading back toward the top of the cover and home. If I'd had a tie I would have thrown it away. A tweed coat would have been in tatters. So much for hunting on a higher plane.

The cow road took us to the brushy overflow.

"I think the crossing is over here in this cluster of young growth," I said, taking the lead, balancing myself along a dark log that took me to a small puddle. "This is it; from here we just hop from hump to hump until we get to the hard ground."

I turned to the log and got my balance. Just then, at that very moment, a grouse that had been hiding in the swamp grass lost its head and rose up for the circle of evening sky over the little pond. Up and up it climbed in a clean, straight, crescendo, followed by the barrels of my deadly old Parker. When they passed its head I slapped the trigger. A tongue of fire licked out and a dark shape fell out of the sky, into the pond. *Ker splash!*

"Hey!" said Bill. "Did you just shoot a duck?"

"Nope, I shot a grouse, and its now floating in this little pond."

"Will Salty go get it?" he asked.

"Nope; Salty doesn't do water. I'll have to reach it with a stick. Here, take my gun." I handed Bill the old Parker and broke off a long sapling.

Slowly and carefully, I inched out on my log, extending the stick like a rake to bring the floating grouse to where I could reach it.

"Got it. Now I have to draw it in. Okay, let's see if I can grab it." I held a light alder tree with my left hand and stretched out as far as I could with my right hand.

Too far. My foot slipped and, like the grouse before me, I fell into the pond. *Ker splash!*

"Heh, heh, heh," came the snickering from the darkness. "Did you get another *duck?*"

"No, I didn't!" My legs oozed down and down until I got them under me. Then I reached out, picked up the soggy grouse, and stuffed it in my vest. The water was two inches deep on top of hip-deep, cold, black muck.

"Give me the guns," I said. "I'll pass them to you on the other side." Bill handed both doubles out of the gloomy brush. His beard was dark, but a bright, toothy grin was easy to see.

The black water pumped out of each boot as I walked up the town road. Salty led the way, moving lightly on her feet, glad to be finished. The muck had painted my legs, making a high-water mark of black mud from just below the side pocket on my left leg to the belt line on my right. Bill moved up alongside. He pointed to the back of the truck. Michael was standing, leaning on the staff, the coffee Thermos open on the tailgate, the happy line of broad grin in his white beard.

"Looks like Moses," Bill said. And, he did, in a rumpled sort of way.

"The survivors of the lost battalion," Mike responded. He pulled his crutch in and saluted smartly. "I heard all the shooting. Any casualties?"

"Just to the birds," I answered and showed him the water-logged specimen from my game bag. Bill lifted out the Kevlar grouse and held it up by its broken wing.

"He ought to be bigger to have caused that much damage," remarked Mike. "The cut on Bill's face looks as if it could use some stitches. How did you manage to get in mud up to your hip pocket?"

"Well, this *is* a gentleman's sport," I answered.

We were a worn-out lot and looked the part. Bill sat on the tailgate and probed the cut with a paper towel. Mike remained mostly upright, leaning on the staff, and I rested against the fender, spattering mud drops on the ground beneath me. The moon rose behind us, so bright that the change from evening into nighttime was almost imperceptible.

A truck came up the town road and turned in at the iron gate. The driver shut off its lights and motor, stepped out of the cab, and walked over to us. He was a strongly built young man with knee-high dairyman's boots and a wrinkled cap advertising a feed company. He asked if we had permission and once assured that we did, he paused and looked us up and down. A question was on his tongue, and he decided to ask it.

Spitting to one side, he asked "Whereuv you boys been, coon huntin'?"

Peals of laughter echoed across the field as the young farmer shook his head and walked back through the gate.

CHAPTER FOURTEEN
Edwin's

His laugh was like the squeaking of bedsprings. His faith, unto death, was in his homestead, It was his life's work, and it was to be that of his sons. But it would come to no end that he could have imagined.

Edwin was born the son of Christ and Elsie Knutson, who settled the land and gathered the fieldstone. With the stones, Christ built the house and laid a foundation for the barn—and for generations to come. To the north and the west, around the farm, runs the course of Stony Brook. No other name would suffice. Every spring, Edwin would say it was possible to walk across his land "from side to side and not touch the ground." If the land forms the man then, by association, Edwin Knutson should have had a heart of granite and a spirit as pinched as the earth between those rocks. But, instead, it was a necessity of his nature to love difficult things, to work at softening the hard corners, smoothing the bumps, and filling the holes. The grinder became the gem, polished—in turn—by the friction, until he was finished and lying in the cow yard behind the barn, failing to answer his wife's call from the back door: "Edwin, come on in."

He was built like a long-shanked skeleton key, with a green feed cap, both ear flaps down. The driveway led between the house and barn, and then to the right-hand side of the machine shed, through the windbreak, and out into the hay field. I always drove slowly, hoping to catch a moment of Edwin's day so I could stop and visit. Sometimes he would be working on his mostly Ford tractor. The framework was Ford —I recognized the hood and grille. In back, he had spread the wheels for a longer stance with parts from something else. When this hybrid machine rolled across the lumpy pasture, it moved with a wide-splayed gait, just as Edwin did. It probably squeaked and wheezed, too, and, that was the whole purpose in stopping to talk to Edwin—just to bounce on the bedsprings of his laughter.

The farm was 320 acres, eight forty-acre tracts in two rows, one row in front and one in back. Four of the forties were cleared, and the remainder consisted of mixed hardwoods, wet lowland, and rock-strewn pasture. The state of Minnesota owned the trees beyond the farm. The land technicians had not been idle: a patchwork of clear-cuts intersected Edwin's bull pasture on the far west side and wrapped around the farmland, enclosing the course of Stony Brook. These were "winter cuts," a term used to define wood gathered when the swamp ground was frozen and easily crossed by tote trails. Once cleared, the land was left to its own devices, a knotted bundle to be sorted out by the foot hunter.

Edwin kept two red bulls in his far west pasture. Neither one ever gave me a second look. They didn't have to. I made sure I couldn't be seen. The first order of business in dealing with the bulls was to locate them, then plan a trip around that location. The passageway into the state ground was right in the middle of the fence on the far side of the open ground. The old story of the two bird hunters gained real-life dimensions.

"Why you taking off your boots?" one said to the other.

"To put on these running shoes," his partner answered.

The fellow laughed, "Why? Don't you know you can't outrun a bull?"

"Don't have to," came the answer.

"Then why put 'em on?" asked the questioner.

His partner stood up, "I only have to outrun you!"

The walk was well worth the risk. The old trail was the winding connection between all the cuts, a narrow hallway of hip-high grass and weeds leading from one old log landing to the next. On both sides the poplar had sorted itself into age classes and sizes that said, "Grouse live here." More important, the trail gave a hunter a place to start from and return to. The cover was immense. A man could be lost a long time in this kaleidoscope of trees.

I got mildly confused one afternoon. My plan was to come

down into the state land from the north instead of entering through the bull pasture on the south. Things went well, I moved a few birds, and I tied some of the old clear-cuts together in a pattern of edge-walking that avoided the low ground of Stony Brook. Looking back on it, now, I realize where I went wrong. The tall grass during that dry fall would have been a wet stream in an ordinary year. I was drawn along by the open patches of blue sky. Walking and circling, flushing up grouse, hunting happily through the peninsulas of old trees, I expected to be turned by the waters of Stony Brook. I walked right on across, helped along by a bird that flushed straightaway in the chest-high mass.

I tipped it, feathering the left wing with a snap shot. Both dogs, the setter and the Labrador, were somewhere out in front. I had a pretty good mark on the drop because the grouse brushed the limbs of some low alders on the way down. So, letting my feet take care of themselves, I stepped along quickly, keeping my eyes fixed on the bushes. The land rose higher, and so did my frustration. The first dog back was Salty. She'd had no contact with the downed bird and had, long ago, learned that a shot does not equal a grouse. She resolved to stay out of my way. Jet followed in a minute or two. Retrieving was what she liked best. Round and around we went, scuffling and snuffling the matted tangle. No luck. I kept walking in ever-widening circles until, by chance alone, I bumped into Salty. She was on point.

"Oh, good deal!" I said aloud. "Whoa girl, hold him." I stepped to her side; she released and quick-stepped another ten yards. I did the same, and she followed suit until we, in the manner of knit two and purl one, had worked our way into a thick, tight spot. That done, the fugitive grouse ran out the other side— and into Jet. Feathers flew and branches shook until the Lab returned happy and wagging with her disgruntled bird, which was wet, spittle-soaked and head up, clamped firmly by both wings. "Good girl, good girl, hold him." I took the grouse from her, carefully gripping it in the same way.

A wounded bird. No grouse ever died of old age, and this one would not feed the foxes, either. I suppose there are politically correct ways to administer the *coup de grace*. Blindfold and cigarette aside, no movie has addressed the issue. When the dog brings the bird all loose and flopping, the circle is complete. A shotgunner can take pride in the perfect execution of his task. Even a dying grouse can be held until its life runs out between the hunter's hands. But a wing-tipped game bird is still whole and, except for its obvious handicap, it would fly or run if released. Its mortality is assured; as for us, it is only a question of time.

Look deeply into its eye. The grouse does not look back. Some species do. I once found a wing-shot hawk, a bird for which I feel as deep a respect as I do for the grouse. It returned my gaze, eye to eye, with a glare of unrelenting defiance. In contrast, the grouse looks beyond its captor, around him, absent of malice, without emotion or recognition. Some speak of a bird suffering. I have held hundreds of them, and never—not once— have I sensed that element. I have, on the other hand, held wounded men, eye to eye, and I know what suffering is.

I think that emotion is only the hunter's. The bird does not care. To finish what started with a shot, badly done, is my duty. How I go about it is my personal choice. I cannot take the bird by its head and spin it about like a nightstick on a tether. Call it bad style or lack of respect, I don't care for the look of it. On the other hand I don't want to study the task so closely as some, learning where to insert the sharp end of a wing quill into the vertebrae behind the bird's head.

I held this grouse firmly and, lifting the gun stock up, I cracked its head smartly against the wood. Done. I looked once more into its eye. It was the same.

I put the bird into my vest and looked around. I was lost. Not exactly *lost*, just misplaced. Another patch of open sky beckoned, and in a few yards of heavy pushing the dogs and I came out into a flat, open log landing. The grass here, however, was trampled down. The large end of a tree sticking out from a pile of tops and branches invited a rest. I rummaged around in my vest pocket for pipe, tobacco, and matches, and in a minute I had a good cloud of smoke floating around.

"Somehow, some way, dogs, I have been here before."

I spoke not in the way that the old hunting guide answered his client's question about where they were: "Well, sir, we're lost, 'cause every time I been lost it looked just like this." I had the feeling that this place with the trampled grass was like another spot on the far side of Edwin Knutson's, up on the state land. But, that couldn't be because I hadn't crossed the brook.

A couple weeks before, Bill and I had taken the left-hand fork of the state-land trail and had walked its entire length. It had ended in an opening just like this one. The place was unusual for two reasons. First, the grass was trampled down, as it would be if several animals had milled about. Second, there were shards of bone scattered around. Bill and I had commented on the behavior of our dogs. Instead of poking and exploring as was their custom whenever we took breaks elsewhere, they had stayed close to us and had looked nervous.

Bill had picked up a piece of heavy bone and turned it in his hand.

"Look," he had said, holding it up for me to see, "toothmarks. This bone has been gnawed by a dog—or a wolf." He had tossed it aside, and the bone had bounced once, landing behind a log.

That log had looked like the one I was now sitting on. As before, both dogs were awake and lying close by. If I was sitting in the same place, then the bone would be right behind me, and I had crossed Stony Brook, somehow, without stepping through water.

"Even worse," I said out loud, "I would be about a mile from where I wanted to be." I turned around, brushed the grass aside, and picked up the bone. Oh man, home was a long ways away!

I tossed the bone away. It had been part of something big and had been eaten by something big. Last year, Edwin had watched a timberwolf ambling across his pasture. He had done what all cow men of his generation do when they see one—he dug out his deer rifle. But, Edwin could not find the cartridges. I had never seen a timberwolf in the wild, but the opening was a long way from any man, and a pack could sleep here undisturbed and without trouble.

"C'mon dogs. It's a long way home with very few birds for entertainment." I tapped out the pipe on the log, closed the little 20-gauge double, and merged into the poplar wall. It closed behind me, a curtain on the first act of a play that would reopen a week later.

The right-hand fork of the state land trail bends back toward Edwin's farm. When it leaves the last log landing, the trail splits and runs on each side of an island of brush and young poplars. My old friend Spence Turner had come with Bill and me on the tour. We had lots of dogs. Hunting with Spence always means a smorgasbord of bird-chasers. Salty, originally one of his pups, was along. So was Jet, Bill had his springer spaniel, and Spence brought one of Salty's littermates, as well as another English setter. We had dogs enough to sell, to rent, to mortgage, to give away to the poor. Spence loves dogs.

A grouse flushed from the island, on Spencer's side. It was his first chance of the season. As the bird climbed up above the tumbling pack, Spence snapped a shot at it. I was swinging on it myself from the other side and, just as he shot, the grouse rolled sideways. From Spence's side it looked like a hit. From my side it was a shot missed. But at almost the same moment, the hapless grouse flew smack into a tree trunk. It dropped, senseless, on my side of the island. The dogs dove into the brushy tangle, tails wagging, Spence urging them on with "Hunt daid! Hunt daid." (Spence is from Missouri.)

I walked about three or four steps and picked up the bird, which was as punch-drunk as a prizefighter. I put its feet in my hand and stood it up. There it was, upright in my palm, gripping my fingers, its mouth slightly open. It was my own pet "parrot," perfectly healthy, a tapestry of brown, tan, and black. This was a singular moment—one not to be wasted.

Bill came out of the brush from my side and was about to ask if anything had fallen when he saw the grouse standing, supported by my hand. Just as he opened his mouth to ask the first question, I put my finger up to my lips. In the meantime, Spence urged all the dogs back and forth through the little isthmus: "Hunt daid, hunt daid!" Bill and I sat down on a convenient log with our backs to the whole production.

The grouse was content to stand quietly and regain its wits. Bill happily filled his pipe and lit it, and I waited for the other shoe to fall, so to speak.

"Hey!" Spence called. "Did either of you see that bird fall? It should be right here!"

"Yeah," I said, "it fell over by me."

"Did one of the dogs get it?" he asked.

"Ah . . . no," I answered.

More scuffling and digging. One of Spence's setters popped out on our side, saw the grouse standing in my hand, and locked on point.

"Spence, you have a point over here."

"Oh," said Bill, his head shaking back and forth, "that's evil."

"Can't be helped, and it's true," I answered.

I moved the grouse to my left hand and lowered it to the log between Bill and me.

Spence plunged through the island. (Spence Turner never walked in the woods; he rolled, like a tank or a bulldozer.) "Where is the point?" he asked.

"Right there," I said, indicating with my right hand.

"He's pointing at you, Bill. Have you got the grouse?" he asked.

"What did the bird look like?"

"What did he look like? He looked daid!" answered Spence. "I shot him, and he fell daid."

"Oh, then it can't be this bird," I said, slipping my palm under its feet. "Because this one is alive." Perky as a chicken, the grouse stood in my hand, the comb on its head erect and its mouth closed. All the little stars, planets, and tweety birds that the cartoonists love to draw around stunned characters suddenly cleared out.

It was time to go! The feet pressed down, and I lifted up the bird at the same time. Like a falconer releasing his favorite hawk, I sent the grouse into the air. It banked hard to the left, past Bill, through the island, and down the road, closely pursued by two white setters.

Sometimes words fail. Spence couldn't form them, and Bill and I couldn't speak. The laughing had taken the explanation away until we could regain our breath. The dogs came back at about the time I finished my story. It was worth a lot more than one dead bird would have been.

The state-land trail ends at the grass pasture of Edwin's neighbor. It was our custom to cross under the fence and then walk the edge back to Edwin's pasture, pausing to let the dogs drink their fill from a cattle pond. The humpy grass tops of an ash swampland signaled the border surrounding a hill. Not just any hill, this one was the source of much strategy and scheming. Beyond it was the bushy and berry-filled pasture along the hay field. In between the pasture and the hill lay a hollow so filled with gray dogwood berries that it would have been possible to harvest them with a farm implement.

Over the years, many councils of war were held to devise ways to drive the grouse from their stronghold and up into the open bushes of the pasture. Likewise, we developed tactics for enveloping the flushed birds and finding them in the hardwood tangle once they scattered. I don't recall any plan that ever succeeded more than once, and even then, the moment lasted only as long as it took to point, flush, and retrieve just one grouse. After that, things would just get, well, out of hand.

It made great material for stories, told on the tailgate as the sun set over the bullpen on the west, casting red rays and long shadows over Edwin's green-hay meadow. These were some of the best times of my life—and all for the sound of a laugh like the squeaking of bedsprings.

CHAPTER FIFTEEN
The Wolf

Yet the wolf eats
He hunts in the darkness
And stays warm
He gets on out there

—Barry Holstun Lopez

He calls it the conversation of death, that moment of eye contact between wolf and prey. For Barry Lopez, author of the book *Of Wolves and Men*, when it happens between two animals, as prey and predator, it is a choice that the encounter will end in death. When it happened to me, it was the most powerful contact I have ever had with a wild creature. The wolf took my stare and turned it back on me. A wolf's eyes tell you that everything evil did not drown in Noah's flood.

The first sign of the great predator was the deer skeleton in the center of the state-land trail, just a few yards west of the brushy island where I had played catch-and-release with Spence Turner's grouse. The buck hadn't gone down easily. The grass was flattened in a circle of torn sod and hair. I turned his skull over with the toe of my boot; it was still attached to the spine and rib cage, and was almost clean of flesh. There were six points, three on each side. The hindquarters were gone; the rib bones and vertebrae stripped clean. I picked up the skull, it was split.

Perhaps the deer had been arrowed by a bowhunter, slinking away to die on this trail to be picked clean by buzzards. It couldn't be a road kill, dragged in here by a scavenging animal. The county highway was more than half a mile away. Wildlife science has always maintained that the wolf kills only the weak, old, and injured. This buck's antlers were not trophy quality, but they once belonged to a deer that wouldn't have been passed up by any hunter in this area. Comparing the head and ribs to those of deer I have butchered, he was mature and in his prime.

Eliminating human causes, and old age, I judged this to be a good place for an ambush. Three or four wolves lying in wait, some on either side of the narrow choke point, could have jumped out and seized the throat of this deer if he had been chased off the nearby pasture by the rest of a pack. The signs of a struggle were apparent. Wolves feeding peacefully on a road-kill carcass would not have broken off the brush and dug the grass and weeds down to the soil. Buzzards may have picked the bones, but they did not carry away the hindquarters.

Do wolves have this sort of knowledge of the country? Can they plan an attack based on that terrain and their experience with the animals that live in it? Even after hunting the ruffed grouse for over thirty years, I would be the first one to admit that when I found that buck, I had learned almost nothing about them by reading and less than nothing by observation. What I did know had been told me by cattlemen friends and loggers.

Over the last three years, wolf sightings had increased. In the winter preceding this grouse season, a pack of six had taken some beef calves about twenty miles west of the kill site I had discovered. Government trappers had been brought in, and in the passage of a week, four of the six wolves were trapped. A few miles away, a pack had chased a farmer's dog under her tractor while she was hauling hay to her cows. She grabbed the door to the cab of the tractor, opened it, and slammed it shut, hoping to frighten them away. It didn't work; the wolves still pressed home the attack. The farmer screamed and yelled, stopping their pursuit long enough to allow her poor dog to run for the barn. The wolves then gathered in a group and stared at the woman. She shut herself into the tractor cab and stared back. Did they see her up in the metal box? She was convinced they did, because, as she related it, "We met eye to eye."

Barry Lopez writes:

"It is popularly believed that there is no written record of a healthy wolf ever having killed a person in North America. Those making the claim ignore Eskimos and Indians, who have been killed, and are careful to rule out rabid wolves. The latter have attacked people several times."

The biggest animal threat in my bird-hunting world at Edwin's was not wolves but his two red bulls. On one occasion, we wanted to hunt the state land next to Edwin's bull pasture. The state trail began on the fence, and the fence was on the other side of the bulls. I am not a fast runner. Bill was with me that day, and I have never seen him run. Max, who was also with me, may have been on his high school's cross-country team, but he never won any ribbons.

All bulls look mean. Maybe it is the way the flesh folds around their faces or the heavy neck muscles that bunch into massive shoulders. They always look as if they are suffering from a bad hangover. The three of us gathered together in the shade of a pasture oak.

"One is lying down; the other is grazing near him," I whispered.

"Yeah, but both are uphill and in the open," Bill added.

"Looks like about two hundred yards of wide, green pasture from here to the fence," said Max.

"We could go low into the humpy swamp grass. That would give us more space, and the humps might slow them down," I offered.

"The humps might slow me down, too," responded Bill. "I think we ought to go straight and fast right across the hard ground."

"If they chase us, we might be able to make the fence in a quick dash," said Max.

"I think we are overreacting," I said. "We have never had a problem with those two. Why would they waste a beautiful day like this chasing three guys?"

"Okay," replied Bill, "Max and I will walk fast as we can. You lag behind to reason with them."

"We go through this every time," I said.

I slipped the bell off Beans's neck and dropped it in my vest. One of the best grouse covers in the state land was right across the fence. Great clumps of gray dogwood flourished in the sun in a young poplar grove, now thinned to walkable openings between the trees. At the bottom of the hill, a wet seep sponged its way into the Stony Brook watershed. Most of the time the grouse flushed uphill, except when they didn't. Because, after all, grouse are going to do pretty much what they please. And, for that matter, so are the bulls.

"Everybody ready? Let's walk!"

There is a certain point in the bull pasture where it is too far to turn back and too far to go forward. That is where I looked at the bulls. The standing bull merely raised his head to watch. His companion could have been wooden.

"I don't know why I worry." My voice kept time with each footfall. "They only chase cows."

Bill reached the fence first and held the wires open for Max and me. "You worry for the same reason I do. Things could change, and they don't talk."

I took the top wire and Bill's gun, and pressed the middle wire down with my boot. "Well, they aren't lions or some other meat eater with lunch on his mind."

Reassembled at the fence wire, we agreed that I would take the low side with Beans. Max would walk in the middle, while

Bill would hunt the hillside just short of the trail. We could see each other pretty well. When a poplar thicket reaches its maximum grouse-holding capacity it is about fourteen to fifteen years old. By then the saplings have sorted themselves out, the aggressive ones reaching higher than their neighbors to take the sunlight for themselves, the shaded ones dying off.

The bell sounds carried well, for there was only a slight breeze. It would have been better if the wind had been in our faces instead of at our back, blowing the scent into the woods in front of us. But that would change as I finished the low edge and climbed uphill.

It was the change in tempo that caught my attention. Bean's bell was not ringing in a steady working rhythm. It was clanging very fast and coming in my direction. I paused, raising my 20-gauge double. Perhaps he was chasing a flushed grouse that would soon be ripping between the gray poplar poles. I saw him—first his head, low and extended, then his shoulders and flank. He was pouring every ounce of effort into speed. Then I saw why.

Close behind him, perhaps ten yards from his withers, a large, long-haired, gray animal was in hot pursuit. It was a wolf. Beans is fast and in great condition, but the wolf was closing the gap. I yelled and waved my left arm.

"Wolf! Hey! Wolf!"

The beast's head had been extended and turned slightly to one side as if to seize a hamstring on one of Beans's hind legs. When the wolf heard my voice, it snapped upright and slowed. I swung the barrels of the 20-gauge out in front of its nose and

The Wolf

fired a shot, plowing the dirt and leaves in its path. It never occurred to me, then, to shoot the animal. The wolf stopped broadside, lowered its head, and focused its eyes on mine.

We had a conversation: "Are you my prey, or am I yours?" A communication between two of the lesser gods, exchanging information through the gaze of one animal into the other. The wolf made a palpable connection, for the hairs on my neck rose. What part of me was speaking to it? Nothing I could sense on my side, yet there the animal stood—not advancing, yet not fleeing. Our kind had spoken before, and that conversation was happening again. We had to make a choice, this wolf and I.

It turned away and walked toward Max. I remembered that I had one shell left in the 20-gauge. I knew—and the wolf had told me—that it would not be enough. Almost entirely gray, with black tips on his ears and eyes, the wolf was at least twice the size of Beans. It stopped in front of Max, then moved on to Bill and stopped again.

At this point, a second curious thing happened. Bill fired both barrels of his shotgun above the beast. In response, it trotted away. It did not run, dodge, or evade. It just trotted away.

Beans came back, panting and shaking. I ran my hands over him; he was not cut or harmed. Bill and Max came downhill to where I was petting the dog.

Bill had opened his shotgun breech and was replacing the two fired shells in a pensive, brooding manner. He tapped the last one around the edges of the left chamber, finally dropping it in as if it was a thought. "That was something," he said.

"It came after Beans, I shot in front of it, then it walked up to you guys. It wasn't scared, not for a moment." I shook my head. "I didn't like that a bit, wild things are supposed to run away."

"If Beans had been old Salty, she would have been dead," said Max.

"That's right. The wolf knew we were near, could hear the bells, could smell all three of us. None of it meant a thing," I said.

"Why didn't you shoot him?" Bill asked.

"I don't know, why didn't you?" I responded.

"I guess I've had it drilled into me that wolves are special, untouchable," Bill answered.

"Do you think there's more than one?" Max asked.

"I think that we have the answer to the flattened grass and the deer skeleton at the end of the trail. Yes, I think there is a pack," I replied.

"Well, we're kind of caught in a spot," said Bill. "The bulls know we are here, so I'm not crazy about going back out that way, and we don't know if there are more wolves waiting on us out this way."

"Let's keep the dog in tight and walk the trail. Once we get to the pasture on the far side, we'll be able to get in the open and walk back onto Edwin's land," I said.

It was easy to keep Beans in close. I didn't see any more of the gray wolf, but the shothair did not want to cast out into the underbrush. We were a few yards short of Edwin's fence when Beans yelped and came running back toward Bill.

"Here we go again!" I said. "Beans! Come!" He was right beside me.

"Max, cross the fence," I told my son. I took his gun from him and handed it back when he was on the pasture side. "Now watch over our backs." Bill and I placed our guns on the ground under the wire and stepped over, picking them up again in one smooth move. We backed up into the open grass and stood for a minute.

"I'm a little jumpy," I admitted. "I guess I don't know what we're dealing with, and until I do, I'm watching my back."

We had walked the cattle pasture all the way back to Edwin's fence, avoiding even our favorite walk through the gray dogwood hole. Once on the other side, we sat down, Bill and I smoked our pipes, and the three of us laid plans for assaulting the bushy clumps between us and our trucks. We were relaxed and happy once again. Nothing had changed in the look of the land, but, something had been added. Something that wasn't there before: fear. There was another predator out there, and it wasn't afraid of us. It didn't understand that I was the top of the food chain.

The wolf had said, "Prove it!"

That experience inspired me to study what is known about the timberwolf. I hoped to learn two things. First, why my dog was attacked and, second, what I could do to keep it from happening again. The answers were unsatisfactory. I learned that very little is known about this animal. What knowledge does exist has been gathered in an effort to hunt down wolves more efficiently. The relationship between wolves and men is old and generally framed by the gunsight. The conclusion of my reading was the same as that of the researchers: We know what wolves are, but we know nothing about them.

There isn't much middle ground when it comes to timber-wolves in my neighborhood. They were hunted to extinction in every state but this one, and here they were driven to the most remote places on the Canadian border. They were trapped, poisoned, and shot from airplanes for bounty and sport until a wolf sighting was worthy of note in the local paper. Those wolves, and the men who killed them, are gone.

But a new generation of wolves came back. Upscale urban-dwellers fuel the new fad for wolf sculpture, art prints, and soul-mate appreciation. On the other hand, I have never seen such art on the walls of hard-rock beef ranchers. They put up seed-company calendars because they are free; there are no wolf pictures on them. These ranchers feed their livestock and expect to lose a few to weather or accident. They don't feed wolves, and don't shoot them or, if they do, they don't brag about it. Wolves have been protected. Whether you agree with that or not it has had one clear result: The timberwolf no longer fears man.

Man is supposed to be the alpha predator, the animal from which all other animals, whether meat or plant eaters, flee upon sight or smell. This arrangement keeps things neat. Unless a hunter seeks to put himself in the way of a toothy tiger, he doesn't have to look to his back. But, as simple folks, we who hunt birds with dogs would like to know something:

Now that the wolf has returned, who is supposed to flee?

Bob White

CHAPTER SIXTEEN
An Estate for Life

When asked whether it is better to marry or stay single, Socrates replied, "Whichever you do, you will regret it."

Edwin married twice. When the first marriage was over, he had the farm, in his name alone; the stone house; the barn; four children; and a steady job running a corporate dairy farm in Michigan. The children grew up and stayed in Michigan, and Edwin came back to Minnesota. He married again—this time to a woman with grown children of her own—and moved back to the family farm. His dream was to make something of the place and bring in his eldest son to farm with him, as he had done with his own father. To that end he labored with the quiet persistence that was his benchmark.

The dairy herd became beef cattle. The best tractor Edwin owned was the same one he and his father had bought new in 1955. If anything was new, he wore it out. If it busted, he fixed it. If it was unrepairable, he kept it for parts. New calves became old cows. The great day came, and he and his son made plans—in my law office—for the passing of the tradition. It was his dream.

It was not his second wife's dream.

As surely as Edwin was connected to his shadow on a sunny day, so also, as the law stated, was he tied to his spouse's hand. The deed of a married man requires two signatures. That's because the interest of a wife, though not stated in the black letters of ownership, is an interest in land as firm and as long-standing as the rocks in its walls. And, though not a single stone was laid by her hand, this woman's twenty years as Edwin's mate translated into 50 percent of his property by law. The deed remained in his file, absent her signature.

Regret, if he allowed himself the luxury of it, was not a chip on Edwin's shoulder. He had made his choices, and he would live with them. The year before he died, he built a wooden scaffold—but unlike any I had ever seen. It was, in my opinion, the perfect manifestation of his hope.

Edwin wanted to paint the barn, fix its roof, and repair the siding. This was not a job for a ladder's narrow rungs. The hay wagon became the foundation. On top of it, Edwin nailed a concoction of boards and slabs reaching to the airy heights of the gabled peak. He created an ancient siege tower of creaky and swaying planks scavenged from piles of old sawn lumber. The Roman legions would have stared in amazed silence, stunned that such a dog's breakfast could stand, let alone move about. It was Edwin's monument to an unquenchable belief that, by his effort, good things would happen.

"Edwin," I said, the first time I saw the scaffold, "somewhere in this state, right now, an engineer of the Occupational Safety and Health Administration is telling his coworkers about a nightmare he had. When he describes what he saw, it will look just like this."

"*Squeak, squeak, squeak, wheeze!*" The happy bedspring laughter of Edwin Knutson rewarded my little metaphor. That, really, was all I wanted, for Edwin had faith. In this place, he could come to no harm. That thought carried him, without regret, to his end. He was not harmed. Edwin died where he wanted to die, doing what he wanted to do: feeding his cattle.

I am now a *persona non gratis* in this place. Unlike Edwin, on occasion, my job does me harm. I am the attorney for his children. When I finished with my fight to carve out their heritage, one hundred sixty of the three hundred twenty acres remained in the Knutson family, subject to an estate for the life of Edwin's widow. The remaining land will probably be sold. Upon her death, the homestead—stone house, barn, pastures, and woods —will return to Edwin's children.

An estate for life. She cannot sell it, but she can mow the lawn. She does not have to paint the barn or even wash the windows. Edwin's second wife is an uneasy trustee for children she neither likes or has reason to help. She is a caretaker without pay. I confess to being a student of irony. I wrote these words, earlier, as descriptive of Edwin, and I find them to be poignant and apply them to her as well: "Faithful unto death to the life of her work, to no end that she will know in this world."

I also have an estate for life on this land, but it has ended. I will be too creaky to hunt birds when I am once again welcome inside these fences. But, when all else is gone our experiences remain, and I have had a lifetime's worth.

For me, Edwin's farm divided itself into three separate, and different, grouse covers. The stone house was, more or less, in the middle. To the right, a mixed collection of hardwood pasture surrounded a low ash-tree swamp. The fence was electric powered. Of just two wires, the top one was barbed; the underwire was plugged into house current. The ash trees stood with their roots in water. This part of Edwin's land could not be crossed on foot. A hill on either side of the ash swamp created a walkable upland dotted with hazel-brush clumps, gray-dogwood thickets, and poplar.

In the middle, behind the house, there was a gate and a fine black-trunked maple tree. It shaded a long rock wall that ran from the barn, stretching back across the pasture. A road for firewood hauling and other chores led from the gate to the electric fence, separating the hardwood hills from the adjoining meadow. The middle ground offered, by far, the best shooting. It was where the grouse gathered to loaf and joke. The grass underfoot was short and green, with lots of clover. Big, dense clumps of brush joined their tops at about head height. The pathways between these islands were about the right height for a grazing cow. The effect was a maze of tunnels and small openings in a matrix of stiff branches. If you hold a hairbrush up to the light and look through it, focusing where the bristles attach to the handle, the appearance would be about the same.

The remaining one-third was the wet, lush border surrounding the balance of Edwin's pasture over to the bull pen. He had cleared everything up to the swamp. A belt of trees, dry humps, and wet holes lay between the pasture and the cattails beyond. Two men and a dog could walk this border land and experience fast, open shooting all the way to the bull pasture.

While I have had wonderful experiences in every inch of it all, by far the most memorable was the day my short, round friend Spence Turner danced with the electric fence.

Samuel Johnson was an eighteenth-century English writer and a man of about the same height and girth as my old friend Spence. He said, "Almost every man wastes part of his life attempting to display qualities which he does not possess." Like its author—and Spence Turner—this comment is both pithy and short.

Spence Turner has no pretensions. Like the earth he is so close to, his qualities are obvious, and display is not in him. Most of his troubles come from association with manmade things like cars, doorways, and electric fences.

The electric wire on Edwin's farm is a sizzler. A companion and I crossed the fence where it borders the far edge of the middle ground. His dog, for reasons of curiosity or bad luck, stuck her nose against the lower wire. The effect was instant and eye opening. She leaped backward and rolled over once. Regaining her feet, she ran for about ten yards, then stopped and looked back at her owner as if he owed her money. She knew about shock collars, and she was bright enough to know that she did not have one on. So, in her mind he had somehow lit her up without one and for no reason. Profuse apologies and cajoling were useless. She had been done wrong. Without so much as a look back, she headed up the trail and spent the rest of the morning under the car.

Spence knew about the live wire. First of all, I had told him about it, and secondly, he had been there the day of the wrongful electrocution. He gets single-minded about woodcock, however, and in the low ash woods, right next to the fence, the woodcock hunting is wonderful. I had already crossed the fence and was walking parallel to him in the close-cropped cow pasture. When the water level got close to the top of Spence's boots, he moved over to the edge.

It is easy for me to step over the wires. At six feet, the notch between my legs is thirty-three inches to the top of my foot. Where I crossed, the ground was hard packed. All I had to do was place my gun on the far side, depress the top wire slightly, and swing over. Spence was on soggy soil at the foot of the hill. where fence wires are higher. In addition, he is lower between the ground and the bottom of his "notch" than anyone I know.

What Spence saw was the top wire at about mid-belly height. He was already over on the other side—in his mind. Unfortunately, where the eyes go, the rest of him had to follow. Spence opened his gun, took out the shells, and bent over to slide under the top wire. The gun and lead arm went through fine, followed by one leg. But when the lead foot touched the ground, the boot sunk in, and the live wire did as well. Spence was bent double, under the top wire, with one foot on each side of the electricity when the charge hit him in a very private and sensitive part of his anatomy.

"Yeow!" he yelled and tried to straighten up. The top wire bounced him back down on the electric wire.

"Yeow!" he yelled, rising up again and being knocked down, with the same result.

"Yeow!" and "Yeow!" and one more time, until he toppled over the fence into the pasture.

"O-o-o-oh, man, that hurts!" Spence moaned, holding the offended appendage tenderly. He rolled over and looked to where I was standing. I wasn't there. I was down on my hands and knees laughing, unable to draw a breath. Really deep, wonderful laughing just rolls me up. Try as I might, I could not form words. The best I could do was extend my hand and wave it up and down in a poor imitation of his acrobatics.

"Well!" he said indignantly, "You're a helluva lot of help!"

Spence was right, of course. I was helpless. He gathered his gear—and his dignity—and walked, in a pigeon-toed sort of way, to our meeting with our mutual friend Bill. There was to be no sympathy from that quarter, either. Bill had seen the whole thing from a high vantage point about a hundred yards away. Spence thought Bill was sitting on the ground taking a rest, but he knew better when he saw Bill's shoulders bobbing up and down as he threw back his head in a guffaw and fell over.

I wasn't too far behind my stout, wire-fried friend when Bill straightened up. Our eyes met and I moved my hand up and

down. He doubled up and said a garbled few words, ". . . needs
. . . rubber . . . underwear." It started all over again.

The middle ground at Edgar's was hunting ground. A covey
of grouse lived in the tunnels and clumps—at least a dozen birds.
They did their dining in a half-acre basin, filled to the brim with
gray-dogwood bushes loaded with berries. Once their crops were
full, the flock would wander under a fence and uphill into the
loafing ground, to spend their day sheltered from overhead pred-
ators by the knitted overstory of brush. Their advantage was in
numbers and heavy overstory.

Bill and I planned and schemed, adjusting our strategies for
wind and weather. We circled the basin, holding the dogs in
tight, winding our way through the woods to creep up on the
back side of the dogwood thicket. The goal was to move the
group up into the middle ground. Once the birds were scattered
among the brush and trees, we would be able to take them one
at a time. But, they were never, ever, one at a time. The dogs
would lose their heads, several shots would be fired. Some of the
grouse would go out to the side, some went forward, and a few
flew right over our heads to the back.

The fence would be crossed, and each man was on his
own. Beans could find the birds, but they would not hold.
Once he lost the body scent, the shorthair reverted to his
hound-dog genetics and trailed the birds by footprint. The
brown biddies were fast-movers in the tunnels of the brushy
pasture. They would run and squat. Beans would follow and
point. Point and go, point and go, closely followed by my fast,

crabbed shuffling, until each bird picked its takeoff spot.

It's hard to shoot from a hunched-over position. They never teach that technique in the schools. The basic elements are: hear the bird, see it flying at a hole in the brush, fill that hole with bird shot. Every now and again, it works—often enough that I consider myself to be an expert.

Success in this sort of situation requires a good bird gun. It may be a 20-gauge double—slim, straight-wristed, swirls of dark walnut in the butt stock. Or a pump action with the bluing worn silver. Or perhaps a semi-automatic or an over/under. But in every case the end result is the evolution of the hunter's personal taste and pocketbook. In every case it is an uncommon gun, scratched by brush and carried long hours between each second of action, lightweight and lightning fast.

For a hunter with the right sort of gun, the low border around the cow pasture was pure entertainment. If the other two covers had been hard and frustrating, some relaxation could be taken by exercising the timberdoodles that probed for worms in its rich black mud. I confess that I killed a few in here simply because I could. The points were solid, the flushes wide open, and the shots easy. I suspect that a lot of video film could be made, for the cover just oozed class and color.

Mostly, I chased fugitive grouse from the middle ground. Once the birds got educated to the escape, a good route was right across the wide-open space and down into the low edge. Grouse would not hold well in this soft environment, but it was fun to watch them fly, free of intervening limbs and leaf screens. And the dogs always performed well.

The cows in the pasture bordering the low swamp were not so well-mannered. They liked to lick the sides of my old Toyota and any other vehicle parked out there. These were Edwin's pets, and as a result they were accustomed to fine things.

My longtime hunting companion from Mason City, Iowa, is a man of precise sensibilities. He appreciates engineering. Jerome Biebeshiemer is German. He drives a Mercedes Benz station wagon. This is a bird-hunter's car, not the sport-utility variety that's so common in the malls. It has been pulled from pot holes by old farm tractors. It has been places and done things that would properly be termed as pushing the envelope. It is sturdy, it is square, and it has only one small concession to aesthetics: On top of the hood is the emblem of the Mercedes Benz factory.

Jerome; his old friend, John Baker; Bill; and I had completed yet another strategic sortie into the middle ground. The vehicles were parked in the pasture, for the enjoyment of Edwin's cows. We had probably done all right, and even if we hadn't, there was a cumulative title of more than one hundred years of grouse-hunting experience to temper the disappointment. It was a bright, sunny day; we had cold beer to drink and sandwiches to eat.

The cows retreated when we crossed the fence. My old Toyota had received its usual licking, and as I bent over to pick up a piece of broken-off plastic trim I heard Jerome's voice come from behind my car.

"Those cows washed all my windows, and, by God, they ate the emblem right off the top of the radiator!"

I'll bet the tripe barrel in the slaughterhouse had the sausage-makers guessing when they found that item.

Stuff is just stuff. It breaks down, you throw it away, and you probably never miss it. Each one of us gathers assets. Some of these consist of personal property and some of real property. Regardless, they are only ours for so long as we live. But what we miss when they're gone—really heartbreakingly miss—is all that really matters.

I miss Edwin's.

CHAPTER SEVENTEEN
Lilacs and House Holes

I am told that it is now possible, with satellite technology, to look down upon the earth and see traces of ancient civilization. Archeologists are using this technique to find things that have escaped the closer scrutiny of walking around on the ground.

Still, I don't think they can see the lilacs and house holes from way up there. But I can find them. Grouse like the edge of old homesteads, and I like grouse. In my wanderings behind my dogs' noses I come across the old places and tracks of the old people.

I have asked around. No one can confirm it, but all agree that there must have been a government plan to give every immigrant settler a lilac bush when he filed his claim. I have mixed results on the plum bushes, but there is no question about the lilacs. That explains why all up and down the Mayo Creek and Stoney Brook clearings, there are lilac bushes by every house hole.

I suppose if houses could have sprouted from saplings they, too, would still be on the old farmsteads in yet another water-nourished shape. But they are gone, along with their builders, because, I guess, they lacked roots. Manmade things fall apart without man. The plants and trees go along quite nicely without the pioneers. Those who remain today are also leaving. Bob, Oliver, Edwin, and Geraldine's people are either gone or soon to move to town. No one like them is coming back.

There's a house hole, with lilacs, in the Promised Land. Thanks to an old aerial photo from 1946, I—like a modern archeologist— have looked down upon the old homestead. I have seen it from two thousand feet, in an almost sixty-year-old, 1/120th-of-a-second image frozen in the sky. In this stopped moment of time, the fields are obvious. There are two of them—one just down from the iron gate and the other out next to the creek. There is no pond, as there is today. The water is a small river flowing free of beaver. There is no house, either. It and its people are gone. But the lilacs are there.

What a perfect location. There is a constant breeze, good water close by, and a fine view of a fertile landscape. On a bright spring day I sometimes leave my office and its stress behind, and take a sandwich out to this place in my pickup truck. Time is slower out here. Ducks fly back and forth, the trumpeter swans have made a nest on the beaver lodge, and every now and then sandhill cranes can be heard in the back field. Time, in a clock-work sense, is constant. The small gears or cyber impulses measure each segment precisely and file it away. But that time, like the old house that used to stand in the hole out here, is manmade. The natural clock is not so finely divided. I think that the thoughts and actions of the old people were, likewise, haphazard.

I once took a trip to the Boundary Waters Canoe Area. The first day my son and I paddled with a steadfast and goal-oriented pace. The next day our schedule was not quite so fixed, for we really had no appointments to keep. By the third and fourth days even our conversation was stretched out by long periods of quiet.

After first light, I asked him the name of a lake up ahead, a place that we had marked on our map as a possible campsite. With no watches to look at and no airplanes to cross the sky we had lost the measure of modern time. We came to a portage. He took the packs and I stepped into the water, spinning the canoe up, over my head, and down onto my shoulders for the portage. The distance was marked by steps and breaths, the time by what ever amount it took to get the work done.

When we reached the other side of the ridge, we rested. When we got to the next lake we set our burdens down and rested again. It was only then that Max looked up at me and said, "Wisini Lake."

We loaded the canoe and paddled off.

There is a building in my state capital. It has seven floors of lawyers and business graduates, all gathered together in one rat warren, all working for the good of the state and the taxpayer, I am told. These people all come in one door in the morning, and all go out the same door at night. I can't say I have been on every floor of this building, but the only wild animals in there are in picture frames. The windows don't open to the outside. If any of the people within those walls hear anything at all, it is the tone of computers and pocket change. A lot of land-use policy is formed in that building. None of it is formed in the grouse covers along the Mayo and the Stoney.

There are people in that building whose parents or grand-parents followed the sun up in the morning and down to bed at night. But these children have now graduated from law school or business school and wear suits to work in faraway places. When their idea of outdoors shrinks from the size of a woodlot to four walls, what will the green leaves formed by the creeks be worth? In a world where money is life's report card and when, one by one, no person listens to the wind, will the only birds that they see be the city pigeons? Will the real things fade away and be replaced by the wildlife print?

My grandfather was not a farmer. He was a settler, I guess, in the sense that he got off the train in a small town in northern Minnesota when travel was done by steel rails and deer trails. He was an attorney. Now, attorneys are the most time driven of all professionals: "Time is money, state your business!"

However, he used to talk about the headlong pace of business as beginning with an early-morning rise to catch the train into Duluth. Then there would be a long dinner over bourbon and a good cigar in the hotel, followed by a card game with his oppo-nent and a few other attorneys until midnight. Next morning, he would have a court hearing at around 10:30 or so, a leisurely lunch, and a return trip on the train to be home by mid-evening.

That pattern is a far cry from today's hourly rates and billable hours. Somewhere, the credo "time is money" picked up every-one and pulled them down the modern road.

Time is not money along the Mayo. Living things with their roots in the water have all that they need. The bank will not foreclose upon the dogwood if it fails to come in with a berry crop. The lilac is a deep-rooted shrub; it will weather the storm and the drought.

What will the eye of the observer see when he looks into a new photograph of my cover (and those along the Mayo and the Stoney) some fifty years from now? This land will not host any humans like the old people; I am sure of that. They were gone when I looked in on them through my 1946 photo. I think that he will see the roofs of several homes and no fields. Perhaps there'll be some lawns and landscaped shrubbery, but no clumps of gray dogwood and unkempt alder runs.

Today there is a new addition to the old cover I called the Other Brother. That feckless, lazy piece of ground has sprouted a house. It is a fine house, just on the inside of the big poplar tree where the five grouse sat so openly. The big thickets that those birds escaped into are now a driveway, and the birds' landing place is a garage. Settlers are returning to the land but not to settle it. They leave in the morning, by the clock, and return in the night after a day at the office. Their signs announce to the world that they are here and, more importantly, that I am not. This land is their land. Turn out the lights, bird hunter; the party's over.

But there is a chance that some person, just one—my child or someone else's—has followed a bird dog until the sweet scent of grouse has become the point and flush. Then, perhaps, the quiet bureaucratic cough acknowledging the end of deep roots and long, quiet pauses—and, perhaps, even bird seasons—will, instead, become "I object!"

Bob White

CHAPTER EIGHTEEN
Voices of Lesser Gods

Consider the ruffed grouse—that one single bird, its life with a predictable end as a meal for another animal, rising like a flower from a bulb and dying as autumn's kill. Its existence as an individual might be over, but the garden continues on. Not every bird dies; some individuals will survive. The grouse is a lesser god of the weedy corners, disdaining all human help, clothed in fabulous colors. Wouldn't he be just as useful as a meal if he were plain as a sesame-seed bun?

I think the grouse is a voice. How could any of my children have crossed the bridge from impossible to possible without his thundering flush and twisting turns? Or without the smell of the fall woods, the display of color, the startling rise, and the return of the messenger, loose and lovely in the soft mouth of a bird dog. My children heard the message from a lesser god telling them to listen to the voice in their heart that said "you can do it" and to ignore the noise that said "no."

Consider the bee, described as E. Annie Proulx sees him: "Flying at the window, seeking to enter again the familiar world, but walled off by a malignant force." Like my son, who—at age fourteen—was struggling to be big as a man at six feet, with strong shoulders but with eyes and hands that could not put the shotgun and the bird together. He suffered through to the end of a day in which he would miss, consecutively, eight woodcock and ten grouse over flawless points. In the same day a companion of his same age collected four of five grouse and declined to even shoot at the woodcock.

What did the voice of the lesser god say to him?

It was a day along the Mayo, with a steady breeze from the northwest and a cover of mixed hardwoods and new second growth. A day for perfect dog work and close-rising birds. Max was born to be my right-hand man, but when the parts arrived he got a dominant left eye. He became a gawky, ill-fitted teenager with parts that, from time to time, seemed to go off on a path of their own. Betrayed by his eyes, my son was a natural right-hander who now had to shoot as a lefty.

Still, like any young pup, he was having a good time barking salutes at flying birds. His failure to fill the game bag had to be addressed, however, because I, as the "able and capable bird hunter," could not see the value in missing. I had a limit, but unless Max killed a bird he was going to (somehow) ruin my day.

Another point and another failure. The superb efforts of the dog and the great luck of finding so many chances in one place became a curse. I am sure my son was praying that our able shorthair would not find another bird to point. But, time after time, the dog pointed until Max stopped shooting altogether. He was dejected and miserable, the chief resident in the home of the losers. I could have encouraged him, handed him my unused shells, but instead I took that opportunity to apply correction to his shooting technique. As any drowning man can tell you, the last thing he needs is to be told how to swim.

When I walked over to give my son some more "instruction," I saw his eyes well up with tears. I had carried this thing too far. He was trying as hard as possible to live up to my image, instead of his own, and failing at every turn.

It should have been over. It certainly was for me. I had no idea how to salvage my son from this hell I had made for him. But it wasn't over. I didn't know it then, but the lesser gods were speaking to me, not him. Until that moment, however, I hadn't been listening.

Beans made a final point, facing into a fence line, only fifty feet from the trucks. Time and all the hunters came to a stop. We were presented with a shot—on a bird that could only be a grouse—in low scrubby dogwood. In the class of opportunities, it was going to be nothing less than wide open. It was my son's chance to pull it all together and was also a risk of hideous proportions.

I thought what none of us dared speak: "If there is a small, sympathetic god in this red-eyed day, let Max get this one!"

The boy made a choice. He straightened his shoulders, drew himself up to his full six feet, and walked to the dog in steady, measured steps. He did it all just the way I had taught him: eyes up where the bird would appear, the gun tucked in under his armpit.

GROUSE AND LESSER GODS

The grouse was there and flushed up, broad tailed, gray, black, and magnificent. It cleared the understory and banked slightly left to right. Max shot.

He missed once and then twice.

It may have been an echo of the last shot, but I swear, that time, hope and the held breath of all of us snapped back into the vacuum left when that last grouse sped away. I heard the voices, and I have never been more proud of my son than I was at that moment.

In my time I have heard every word said in a like circumstance. I have seen a grown man, a self-professed icon of the sport, kick his dog breathless. I have said many of the words myself. Yet without a single good example in front of him, and in the face of overwhelming bad luck and unrelenting pressure, my son kept his temper and dignity, and bore the weight with presence, patience, and tolerance.

"Max," I said, "I have never, ever, seen anyone have a worse stretch of bad luck, nor have I ever seen anyone handle himself better. I want to shake your hand."

"But I didn't get anything," he answered.

"You got experience and my respect," I said, "two things that I promise you will last a lot longer than a pile of dead birds."

*   *   *

The devil with a problem is that it comes at you whole and all at once. The answer to the problem, on the other hand, comes in small parts that arrive at odd times. When you least expect it, some small segment of the answer is delivered. Perhaps it's in the form of a paragraph read in a newspaper article. Maybe a friend gives a small piece of advice. Sometimes, while working on an unrelated project, the answer to a fragment of the problem is discovered. Then, one morning you wake up, and there it is! The whole answer.

Time and civilization work against my grouse hunting. Hardly a year goes by that I don't lose a cover to a land sale or aging forage or a deed that gives Suzie five acres so that she can put up a trailer. That is a devil of a problem.

So, in the middle of my life, I decided to put together a map of all the places I hunt grouse and study it a long time. I thought that if I could see the pattern it made, then I would better know where to go next.

The problem I was searching to solve was for more places to kill more grouse. What I learned was that I could not confine the nature of the grouse and where it lives to those limits. The answer was available, but I had to stop thinking like the goal-oriented, type A, anal-retentive human I am. I had to give up my world, where the rules are:

Believe nothing that cannot be proved.
Respect nothing that cannot be understood.
Value nothing that cannot be sold.

The lesser gods, the green leaves, the wind, the whole water brotherhood—all of them—were searching for me. After all, how can I *prove* that the black geese fly by the stars when the stars are behind the clouds? How can I *understand* that the bumblebee flies when science says that it cannot? For that matter, can I put a *value* upon the tight, exciting knot in my stomach when I see a dog on point? None of this advances any stock market nor earns interest. I live in a world where money is life's report card.

The answer is the same as in shooting: trust your instinct; more by faith, less by sight.

Civilization has piled layers and layers of gray matter on top of it, but curled up in a quiet corner of my mind there is the voice of the morning wind, warning of sea storms. There was a time when my ear could divine the pads of a hunting beast. My hair, now so barber cut and dry, was once a messenger of direction when combed by the wind. Inside my chest, in a quiet corner of my heart, in the blood of my body, a part of the water brotherhood lives today. This human form is thousands of years old. Some small element of me has heard all the songs, sailed the cold seas, and survived the storms. I know this is true because I am here today.

If I want to hear the small voices, then I must listen in the quiet. It is a hard thing to do because in today's world it is more important to know the levers and knobs of the big engines. The search is no longer for food and life; it is the quest for money. With money, all the things made by the big engines can be bought. The machine sound is now the sound of survival. If the power fails, the machine noise is gone. Suddenly, everything else that was thought to be mute, docile, and tamed, has a sound. The old voices are always there; they're just overwhelmed by the white noise of progress.

Consider this:

A coin tossed into the air,
the petals plucked from a daisy,
the open pages of a fallen book,
are not read as statistical noise;
but as signs, messages,
a dialogue with eternity.

—Gabriel Zaid

More voices of lesser gods.

Sometimes these ancient voices reach out to me, linking my childhood to who I am and connecting me to the people who went before me. Within them, if the night is quiet and the grass is new, float sounds like spring peepers or perhaps a summer robin or, later in the night, a night hawk. Or maybe there's a siren, if the weekend is busy and the night is hot. In the fall, there might be a dog, a mile away, tied up outside and not happy about it. These are messages for the ears, yet there are times in autumn when the air is lined with shimmering strands of spider silk, as if each tiny creature has suddenly found it necessary to leap into the breeze, sending me a visual message to tempt my fate, attached to a long, single rainbow of thread.

These lesser gods and the beauty of their message are not yet lost to those who will listen.

When I am in my covers and along my creeks, my mind is quiet. I can listen and heed their voices. It's not as if I receive any words. There are no spooky echoes in my head. Rather the feeling is one of being in harmony with everything around me. The way I walk, pause, turn, and stop is not chosen with any conscious thought on my part. A likely looking grouse corner is approached by one direction this day and the opposite direction the next. I am successful both times.

In other places and circumstances, people call that following a "hunch." The whole concept is now an established legal principle called "probable cause." It is nothing more or less than paying attention to the nagging thought in the head and doing what it says. I think that in my quiet mind the "gut reaction" is just being obedient to another will. I have, from time to time, tried to force my thoughts onto the task. It doesn't work.

This year I searched for some new places. I selected each piece of land because it had, on paper, all the necessary logical elements of a place where birds would be found. But within fifty yards or so, I knew by the feeling in my gut that the cover was no good. It had everything that grouse need to get by: trees of the right age and gray dogwood in the right places, but it had no "soul." There was no harmony for me to blend into. Admittedly, I hear what pleases me, and sometimes I don't understand it all at once, so I often spent a couple hours trying to prove my inner voices wrong. But I could hear something after I quieted my mind.

The voice said, "You're wasting your time."

I have other covers that are pretty much birdless, but I don't go there for the hunting. These are just beautiful, spiritual places to be—churches in the natural world. They speak to me and I